98 Ways To
Cook Venison

● ● A Collection of Eldon's Best Venison Recipes.

Author: ....Eldon R. Cutlip
Photographer: ....Eldon R. Cutlip
Cover Photo: ....Eldon R. Cutlip

© Copyright 1997 by Eldon R. Cutlip/Eldon's Game Care and Sausage Fixings, Box 145, Grangeville, Idaho 83530. 1-800-352-9453. All Rights Reserved. Printed in the United States of America. First edition: November 1997. Printed by: Print Craft Printing Inc., Lewiston, Idaho. ISBN: 0-9644 922-3-7. For your free catalog featuring working knives, cutting boards, tenderizers, game care, processing, sausage and jerky making products... call 1-800-352-9453, or write to: Eldon's Products, Box 145, Grangeville, Idaho 83539

Table of Contents

INTRODUCTION

The idea for this handbook came about during our stint at the 1997 Eastern Sports Show in Harrisburg, Pennsylvania. Our booth was crowded with onlookers and my wife and I were knee-deep in serious transactions, serving several customers at once, when a stooped, elderly lady worked her way through the crowd and caught my eye.

"I want a book that's got nothing but venison recipes . . . pot roasts, steaks, meatloaves, a main dish sort of thing!"

The point was well taken, so I've put together a collection of my best venison recipes, compiled from 30 years of trial and error. "98 Ways To Cook Venison" includes the best of "Cooking Wild From Idaho" and a potpourri of long-time favorites.

The recipes take advantage of venison's concentrated flavor by suggesting spice proportions that enhance rather than cover up its exquisite wild taste. The soups and stews are thick and full-bodied. Roasts are seasoned to perfection and cooked in such a way as to produce the best possible flavor and texture for each cut of meat. There's no second guessing which steak to use because each recipe spells out the correct cut for the best results.

I've also included a selection of cured products, recipes such as ham, pastrami, dried venison, etc. The methods are simple and the formulas effective. Each is designed specifically for venison, which is typically leaner and drier than most domestic meats.

Venison is the meat from deer, elk, caribou, reindeer and moose. Antelope meat is akin to mutton and should be prepared accordingly. Bear, on the other hand, is a distant relative of the pig family. The meat should be fully cooked before eating to guard against infection from the trichina parasite which can cause trichinosis in humans.

"98 Ways To Cook Venison" may well be the definitive handbook on venison cookery. Yet, I doubt I could have put it together if it weren't for the 'missus' of over 25 years. She's enthusiastically tasted too many experimental dishes to have kept count, never complaining, always willing to give an objective opinion . . . good or bad. And so I dedicate this volume to Karen and her enormous capacity to try the unknown simply because I ask.

Eldon R. Cutlip

WHAT YOU SHOULD KNOW ABOUT VENISON

Great tasting game doesn't just happen. It's the by-product of good conscientious care which starts the moment an animal is put down and continues right up to the time of consumption. Shortcuts are simply inexcusable. Wild game is too precious to waste. Still, every hunting season there are a number of big-game kills rendered useless because of inept handling practices. Hunters either don't care enough to commit the extra time to game care, or they're not aware of the many variables that alter wild meat flavor. In either case, the following tips, compiled from years of professional game-handling experience, should help you produce first-rate table fare from your next game aninal.

COOLING: Venison (game meat) is extremely perishable, and field conditions are usually less than perfect. The meat must be taken care of **ASAP**. You start by removing the innards, being careful not to puncture the stomach during the process. If it's a large animal, such as an elk or moose, a block-and-tackle can be used to elevate the carcass while you work on it.Otherwise, roll it onto a clean surface, such as a canvas or plastic tarp, to keep the meat clean as you proceed. Remove the skin in the usual manner, sever the head and legs, remembering to cut the front legs off at the knee joints and the back legs off above the hocks so as to leave the rear tendons intact for hanging purposes. Cut the skinned carcass into quarters or convenient-sized pieces (this step is almost impossible without a saw or hatchet). Place the quarters into clean, quality game bags, tie and hang in a shaded area until they can be transported to a meat locker.
NOTE: Whether it's a deer, bear, antelope, elk or moose, the aforementioned process is crucial and should be done immediately. Picture taking and the like shouldn't be allowed to interfere with proper field care. The faster an animal is cooled out, the better the meat!

ELEVATING THE CARCASS: If encroaching darkness or lack of necessary equipment and know-how prevent immediate care, it's imperative you at least open up the carcass and get it off the ground so air can circulate around the carcass and cool the meat. If you're alone, clearly the best option is to roll the big fellow onto a nearby stump or log. When that's done, find a solid stick and prop open the chest cavity. **Assuming the meat is worth more to you than the cape, slit the neck wide open from the chest cavity to the base of the lower jaw.** Completely remove the trachea. Next, split the pelvic bone and carefully cut out the anus and bladder; discard. Tie a rope around a hind leg, secure the other end to a nearby anchor and pull the hind legs apart; tie off. The resulting airflow will help to cool the carcass until you return. **If it's a deer, hang the entire carcass when possible.**

PREDATORS: If you have to leave meat in the woods overnight, it's advisable to hang at least one article of clothing near the carcass to help ward off predators. More than one hunter has had prime elk meat ruined because he didn't think to leave a shirt or jacket in the vicinity of the kill. This trick won't work every time, especially if a hungry bear is involved, but it's usually enough to keep coyotes and cats at bay until you return.

SKINNING: When feasible, game should be skinned while it's warm. Speedy hide removal serves three purposes. First, it allows the carcass to glaze over which helps to prevent wild meat from souring. Secondly, because blowflies prefer to lay their eggs on moist surfaces, it reduces the risk of blowfly infestation. And thirdly, the glazing process helps dry out nuisance hairs so they can be burned away with a propane torch before processing.

REMOVING COPULATORY HAIR: When you're field-dressing a bull elk, it's very important to know that the hair prevalent around a bull's copulatory area (about 2-inches on either side of the scrotum) is exceptionally rank. Even a few strands of this extremely rank hair is enough to taint an entire elk carcass. So extreme caution is advised when dealing with the scrotum. Remove the copulatory hair (hide and all) carefully; discard immediately. **Clean hands and knife thoroughly before resuming the skinning operation.**

TARSAL GLANDS: The tarsal glands, those rank little tufts of hair located on the inside of a deer's hind legs just above the hock, are another potential problem area for first-time hunters. These glands are extremely foul and taint any meat that come in contact with it. You can't scrub the foul odor away and you can't buy enough barbecue sauce to mask its horrid taste. **Cut them off and discard, but don't handle a tarsal gland and then handle the carcass.** Heed experience!

GAME BAGS: I've seen some pathetic looking game bags during my years as a wild-game processor. These cheap replicas are made from a cheesecloth-type material that doesn't repel blowflies, dirt or dung. In addition, inferior game bags tend to hold moisture around wound areas, creating a perfect environment for blowfly infestation. The point is, if you're going to use game bags to protect your meat from field to processing plant, don't waste your money on cheap bags because they're ineffective. If you can't afford good quality bags, then you're better off not to use bags at all. **NOTE: Quality game bags, although more expensive, can be washed and used time and time again.**

BLOWFLIES: Immediately after your game is transported from camp to home (preferably a cold-storage locker), the game bag should be removed so the meat can air out. Next, check the entire carcass for blowfly eggs and remove any you find lest they hatch into adults and render the meat useless.

WATER: Although it's beneficial to flush out the cavity area of your game, **don't use a hose on the outside of the carcass** unless you plan to cut it up right away. And even then, it's a sloppy mess to work with. Moreover, wet meat sours quickly, so you could lose a whole animal if you washed it down and couldn't cut it up right away. **I would suggest you wipe down the carcass with a solution of 4-parts water and 1-part vinegar just prior to processing.**

HANGING: I don't hang wild game more than two or three days, and then only if it's hung in a controlled temperature between 33 and 36 degrees F. Hanging game meat only serves to decrease the net yield. Any improvement having to do with tenderness usually isn't worth the **gamy taste generated by the bacterial breakdown that takes place during the rotting process.**

CUTTING AND WRAPPING: Don't assume anything. Just because you get your deer or elk to a processing facility on a Thursday doesn't mean it will be cut and wrapped by Friday. To be fair and to prevent loss from spoilage, most game processing operations work on a first-come first-serve basis. Obviously, your meat will have to hang a few days before it's finally processed. So it's imperative that you take your deer or elk to the processor ASAP if you expect it to be cut and wrapped while fresh.

GAME TALLOW: Under less than ideal temperatures (33-36 degrees F.), game tallow turns rancid very quickly. As it does, it begins to break down and drip ever ever so slowly down the carcass, covering everything in its path with a thin film of rancid tallow, which subsequently gives the meat a gamy taste. To avoid this potential problem, remove the tallow before you put the animal in storage. First-rate flavor is certainly worth the extra minutes it will take to cut away the tallow.

THIN DEER: Not every deer has excess tallow. In fact, many of the deer harvested each fall are very lean, zero fat, almost anemic by human standards. These "skinny" deer should be examined for festering wounds, boils, sores, spots on the liver, or other visible disorders that might explain their poor condition. If you have doubts concerning an animals health, you may want to have it examined by the local fish and game authorities. If they deem it unfit for human consumption, they may issue you another tag so you can try again for a healthy animal.

Other variables that commonly produce "skinny" deer are old age, over-population, drought and various food shortages due to overgrazing, poor mast crops, fire, etc. Late birthing does may also be on the thin side if they're harvested before they have a chance to recuperate from lactation. **Rutting bucks, particularly the dominant breeders, are very often extremely lean late in the rut.** While most of the thinner deer in the latter categories aren't likely to be as tasty as their plumper counterparts, they still make aceptable table fare. An alternative that makes your skinny deer excellent eating is to process the meat into into burger or sausage.

BONEDUST: If you have your venison cut up with a ban saw, you may want to take heed. The meat/bone/fat residue which accumulates during the cutting process, can, under certain conditions, actually contaminate your meat and cause it to taste very gamy. For example: imagine the prized deer you left at the local processing facility is scheduled for cutting around 6:00 p.m. Figuring the ban saw has been in use since early a.m., and assuming all the deer cut prior to 6:00 p.m. were processed properly, the worst that's likely to happen is that your meat will have an assorted dusting of meat/bone/fat residue.But what if one of those deer was spoiled? **Always insist that all the bonedust is scraped off your meat before it's packaged.**

CUTTING ACROSS THE GRAIN: With possibly the exception of over-cooking, cutting game meat incorrectly is the number one reason so many first-time processors end up with tough steaks. To make matters worse, the problem usually isn't detected until the deer is completely processed and it's too late to remedy the situation.

I would suggest first-time processors take it slowly. First, lay out the muscle you plan to cut; (sirloin tip, round, backstrap, etc.,) and make a thin cut. Secure a good hold with the thumb and forefinger of each hand and try to pull the slice apart. **If you've cut it across the grain, separation is easy. If your cut is with the grain, separation is difficult.** Examine the cuts closely and you'll see the difference in the grains. Test each muscle the same way and, with practice, you'll be able to identify the "run" of the grain simply by looking, just as a professional meat cutter does.

WRAPPING: Single wrapped meat often freezer burns within the first two to three months. Always double wrap your meat to get the longest possible freezer life. For best results, start with a plastic film, and make uniform, airtight packages. Finish up with quality, plastic-coated freezer paper. Again airtight packages are a must. Label and date each package. For maximum flavor, use venison within 8 to 12 months.

GRINDING BURGER: When you're ready to grind your venison burger, you'll probably want to add at least some fat to replace the game tallow you discarded earlier. I always use fresh beef fat, and now that I'm older and more health-conscious, I add 5 percent fat instead of the 12 or 15 percent I used to use. Most hunters add 10 to 12 percent fat which still makes a lean burger, especially when compared to store-bought hamburger.

To Grind: Weigh out your lean meat in an ample-size container and add whatever percentage fat you've decided on. Toss meat and fat together and grind once through the chosen plate. Mix well and grind again. Double wrap or stuff into poly-bags and freeze until needed.

Choosing The Correct Grinder Plate: There are a number of plates to choose from, with the most popular sizes ranging from 1/8-inch to 1/2-inch which is the diameter of the computer-drilled holes. Generally, a 1/8-inch plate is used for fine-ground hamburger, ground (restructured) jerky, bologna, franks, etc. A 1/4-inch plate is good for regular-ground hamburger, salami, summer sausage, pepperoni, snack sticks, etc. A 3/16-inch plate is used for coarse-ground hamburger, breakfast sausage, Polish/Kielbasa, German sausage, boudin, etc. A 3/8-inch plate is often used for the first hamburger and sausage grind, coarse-ground breakfast sausage, linquisa, chorizo, chili meat, etc. A 1/2-inch plate is also used for the first hamburger and sausage grind, chili meat, chorizo, vegetables, cheese, etc.

COOKING: Wild-game meat (excluding bear meat which is prone to the trichina parasite) doesn't have to be cremated to be palatable. **In fact, a medium-rare or medium-cooked venison steak is considerably more flavorful than a venison steak that's overcooked (well done).** Because venison (deer, elk, moose, caribou, etc.) doesn't have the inner-marbling fat consistent with beef and pork, it's much drier to begin with. So when venison is cooked to the well-done stage, it's essentially had all the natural juices and flavor removed, leaving a juiceless, tasteless piece of meat with the same consistency of shoe leather. **I eat all my venison medium-rare to medium and nothing tastes better!**

SUMMARY: To sum it up, poor tasting (gamy) venison can usually be attributed to less than perfect care somewhere between the field and table. Study the aforementioned tips and pinpoint the ones that may have caused past problems. Apply them to your game-care practices the next time you go afield, and no one will say your vension tastes gamy again. **When hunting, think before you pull the trigger. Forfiet any shot that won't produce a clean kill. There's always tommorrow and another chance. And when you score, treat the downed animal with the respect these magnificent animals are due.** *Eldon R. Cutlip*

Seasonings are the key in this recipe. The red wine vinegar tenderizes the venison while providing a nice complement to soy sauce and molasses. Delicious!

TERIYAKI GRILL

8 to 12 wooden skewers
1 pound venison round steak
1/8 cup red wine vinegar
1/8 cup soy sauce
1/8 cup olive oil
1 tablespoon molasses
1 teaspoon ginger
1 teaspoon dry mustard
1/2 teaspoon garlic powder
4 cups hot cooked rice

1. Soak wooden skewers in water for at least 6 hours before starting recipe. This will prevent the meat from sticking to the skewers, plus they're less likely to burn while grilling.
2. Partially thaw venison round steak; slice diagonally across the grain into 1/4-inch thick strips. Set aside.
3. Combine red wine vinegar, soy sauce, olive oil, molasses, ginger, dry mustard and garlic powder in shallow dish; stir mixture well.
4. Add meat strips; stir well, cover and refrigerate 1 to 2 hours.
5. Remove meat strips from marinade and thread carefully onto wooden skewers.
6. Place skewers on grill over medium-hot coals; grill 2 to 3 minutes on each side.
7. Serve over hot cooked rice.

Makes 4 to 5 servings.

Contrary to popular belief, venison doesn't have to boring. Try this stir-fry recipe and I think you'll agree.

SPICY STIR-FRY

1 pound venison round steak
1 tablespoon chili powder
1 tablespoon cayenne pepper
1 beef bouillon cube
1/2 cup hot water
2 teaspoons cornstarch
3 tablespoons olive oil, halved
2 cloves garlic, diced
1 large zucchini, cut into long, thin strips
1 large red bell pepper, cut into long, thin strips
2 large stalks celery, cut into long, thin strips
2 cups whole kernel corn
Hot cooked noodles

1. Cut venison round steak into long thin strips.
2. Sprinkle chili powder and cayenne pepper over meat strips. Toss gently to coat strips; set aside.
3. Dissolve bouillon cube in hot water to make beef broth; add cornstarch, stir well and set aside.
4. Pour 1 1/2 tablespoons olive oil around top of preheated wok to coat sides of wok with oil.
5. Heat wok at medium-high heat (325 degrees) for 2 minutes.
6. Add venison strips to wok and stir-fry 3 to 4 minutes; remove strips and set aside.
7. Pour remaining 1 1/2 tablespoon olive oil into wok; add garlic, zucchini, bell pepper, celery and corn. Stir fry 2 to 3 minutes or until zucchini is crispy tender.
8. Return seasoned/cooked venison strips and beef broth to wok; cook, stirring constantly until thickened.
9. Serve over hot cooked noodles.

Makes 4 servings.

A great menu begins with grilled vension steaks. Add grilled vegetables, a fresh garden salad, oven garlic bread and you have the perfect evening meal for the steak lovers in your family.

HICKORY GRILLED CHOPS

1 to 2 cups hickory (or mesquite or alder) wood chips
1/4 cup red wine
1/4 cup lemon juice
1/4 cup soy sauce
1/4 cup Worcestershire sauce
3 cloves garlic, minced
1 teaspoon white pepper
Prepared mustard
8 (1 1/2-inch) deer chops

1. Soak hickory wood chips in water for 2-3 hours.
2. Combine red wine, lemon juice, soy sauce, Worcestershire sauce, minced garlic and white pepper in shallow dish; stir well.
3. Brush mustard lightly on both sides of chops; place chops in marinade. Cover and marinate 4 hours.
4. Place dampened wood chips directly on hot coals.
5. Place chops on grill rack; grill 6 to 7 minutes on each side or until chops reach desired degree of doneness, basting chops frequently with remaining marinade.

Makes 8 servings.

Although my wife doesn't hunt, she knows that if I'm success-ful, she'll share the benefits. One of her favorite meals includes real mashed potatoes and chicken-fried steak.

CHICKEN-FRIED STEAK

1/2 cup flour
1/3 teaspoon salt
1/3 teaspoon lemon pepper
1 pound venison cube steaks
2 eggs, beaten
3 tablespoons milk
2/3 cup Italian cracker crumbs
1/2 cup vegetable oil
3 tablespoons flour
1 cup beef broth
3/4 cup milk
hot sauce

1. Combine flour, salt and lemon pepper in small mixing bowl; stir together well.
2. Dredge each steak in seasoned flour, forcing as much flour into the meat as possible.
3. Combine eggs and 3 tablespoons milk in mixing bowl; stir well.
4. Dip dredged steaks in egg mixture. Dredge in Italian cracker crumbs; set aside.
5. Pour vegetable oil into a large, heavy skillet; heat.
6. Carefully place steaks in hot oil and cook over medium heat until steaks are browned, turning steaks once to brown both sides. Cover, reduce heat, and simmer 20 minutes, turning occasionally.
7. Remove steaks; set aside. Pour off drippings, reserving 3 table-spoons in skillet.
8. Stir in 3 tablespoons flour, beef broth, milk and 3 or 4 sprinkles of hot sauce, stirring constantly until thickened and bubbly.
9. Serve gravy over steaks.

Makes 4 servings.

When you get the hankering for something different, thaw some venison cube steaks, round up the herbs and create this colorful main dish. Delicious!

HERBED STEAK

1 1/2 pounds venison round or sirloin tip steaks
(cut 3/4 to 1-inch thick)
2 tablespoons olive oil
1/2 teaspoon garlic granules
2 tablespoons dried chives, 1/4 cut
2 tablespoons dried parsley, 1/4 cut
1 tablespoon granulated onion
1 teaspoon basil
3/4 teaspoon salt
1/4 teaspoon cayenne pepper
1/2 teaspoon oregano
1/8 teaspoon thyme
2 tablespoons red wine vinegar
1/2 teaspoon lemon juice

1. Place venison steaks in large, shallow baking dish.
2. Combine olive oil, garlic granules, chives, parsley, granulated onion, basil, salt, cayenne pepper, oregano, thyme, red wine vinegar and lemon juice in an ample size mixing bowl; stir well and pour over steaks.
3. Cover steaks and marinate in refrigerator 4 to 6 hours, swishing/ turning occasionally.
4. Drain excess marinade from steaks; reserve.
5. Rearrange steaks in shallow baking dish. Broil 4 inches from heat 7 to 8 minutes; turn and broil an additional 7 to 8 minutes or until steaks reach the desired degree of doneness.
OPTIONAL: Herbed steaks are also excellent grilled over medium-hot coals.

Makes 6 servings.

Wake up your tastebuds with the great flavor of Cube-Steak Italiano made from fresh-frozen venison. Top off the meal with a fresh garden salad and toasted Italian bread.

CUBE STEAK ITALIANO

2 tablespoons olive oil
4 venison cube steaks (approximately 4 ounces each)
1 medium green bell pepper, chopped
1 medium onion, chopped
1 cup water
1 cup uncooked rice
4 to 5 drops hot sauce
1/2 teaspoon salt
1/8 teaspoon black pepper, table grind
2 (14 1/2-ounce) cans Italian stewed tomatoes, undrained
1 (4-ounce) can tomato paste
Parmesan cheese

1. Heat olive oil in large skillet, add cube steaks and brown on both sides. Remove and set aside.
2. To pan drippings, add bell pepper and onion; cook over medium heat until onion is crispy tender.
3. Add water, uncooked rice, hot sauce, salt and pepper; simmer 5 minutes.
4. Add Italian stewed tomatoes and tomato paste; stirring mixture constantly.
5. Place browned cube steaks in skillet and smother with onion/rice/tomato mixture. Cover; simmer 45 to 50 minutes.
6. Top each serving with Parmesan cheese.

Makes 4 servings.

If someone invites you to their house for venison beer steaks, you'd better not hesitate. Tender and delicious is the only way to describe this unique dish.

BEER STEAKS

2 tablespoons olive oil
1 1/2 pounds venison sirloin tip steaks
2 beef bouillon cubes
1 cup hot water
2 medium onions, chopped
2 cloves garlic, minced
3/4 cup tomato juice
1 (8-ounce) can mushroom stems and pieces, drained
1 teaspoon dried basil
1/2 teaspoon salt
1/4 teaspoon white pepper
4 tablespoons flour
1 cup beer
6 cups hot-cooked fettuccine

1. Heat olive oil in Dutch oven; add sirloin tip steaks. Brown both sides; remove and set aside.
2. Dissolve bouillon cubes in hot water to make beef broth; stir well and set aside.
2. Add onions and garlic to Dutch oven. Cook over medium heat until onions are crispy tender, stirring often; drain.
3. Stir in reserved beef broth, tomato juice, mushroom stems and pieces, basil, salt, white pepper and flour; cook over medium-low heat for 2 minutes or until thickened.
4. Stir in beer. Add reserved steaks, cover, reduce heat and simmer 1 hour.
5. Serve over hot-cooked fettuccine.

Makes 6 servings.

For an easy meal that's guaranteed to please, it's hard to beat a hot skillet of smothered venison sandwich steaks served on bakery-fresh rolls.

SANDWICH STEAKS

1 pound venison round or sirloin tip roast
2 tablespoons olive oil
1 large onion, white or yellow
3 large green or red bell pepper, chopped
1 (8-ounce) can mushroom stems and pieces, drained
1/2 cup mozzarella cheese, grated
1/2 cup sharp cheddar cheese, grated
2 tablespoons Parmesan cheese
1/2 teaspoon garlic salt
1/4 teaspoon black pepper
4 bakery-fresh rolls

1. Slice venison roast into 1/8-inch thick sandwich steaks.
2. Heat olive oil in a large cast iron skillet. Add onion, peppers, mushroom stems and pieces; cook over medium heat until onion is crispy tender.
3. Remove cooked onion/bell pepper/mushroom mixture from skillet and set aside. Add sandwich steaks to skillet and cook over medium heat about 1 minute on each side; drain skillet.
4. Spread cooked onion mixture evenly over sandwich steaks.
5. In a small bowl, combine mozzarella cheese, cheddar cheese, Parmesan cheese, garlic salt and pepper; mix well. Sprinkle seasoned cheese evenly over onion mixture, cover and cook over medium heat for 3 to 4 minutes or until cheese is melted.
6. Remove skillet from heat, uncover and serve immediately on bakery-fresh rolls.

Makes 4 servings.

1. Slice 1 pound (10 to 12) sandwich steaks from the sirloin tip roast. Steaks should be about 1/8 inch thick.

2. Heat olive oil in a large cast iron skillet; add onions, peppers, mushroom stems and pieces. Cook over medium heat about 1 minute on each side or until onions are crispy tender; drain skillet

3. Remove cooked onion/ mushroom mixture from skillet and set aside. Add sandwich steaks to skillet and cook over medium heat about 1 minute on each side; drain skillet.

4. Spread cooked onion mixture evenly over sandwich steaks.

5. In a small bowl, combine mozzarella cheese, cheddar cheese, Parmesan cheese, garlic salt and pepper; mix well. Sprinkle seasoned cheese evenly over onion mixture. cover. Cook over medium heat for 3 to 4 minutes or until cheese is melted.

6. Remove skillet from heat; uncover. Serve immediately on bakery-fresh rolls.

For years, wild-game cooks have insisted that venison be cooked until well-done. But anyone who has eaten venison cooked pink and juicy will attest to its superior flavor.

GARLIC-BUTTER STEAK

1 teaspoon garlic powder
1 teaspoon basil
1/2 teaspoon seasoning salt
1/2 teaspoon black pepper, coarse ground
1 1/2 pounds venison sirloin tip steaks, cut 1-inch thick
2 tablespoons lemon juice
1 tablespoon red wine vinegar
1 tablespoon Worcestershire sauce
1/4 teaspoon hot sauce
1/4 cup butter

1. Mix together garlic powder, basil, seasoning salt and coarse ground pepper.
2. Sprinkle both sides of steak with garlic mixture; refrigerate 2 to 3 hours.
3. Mix together lemon juice, red wine vinegar, Worcestershire sauce and hot sauce; set aside.
4. Melt butter in large skillet; add seasoned steaks. Cook rapidly over medium-high heat, browning each side of steak.
5. Reduce heat to medium, add lemon juice mixture and cook steaks 2 to 3 minutes on each side or until or until steaks reach desired degree of doneness.

Makes 6 servings.

If you're a kabob lover, you're going to love this recipe. The right combination of herbs and spices transforms venison into a culinary delight guaranteed to please.

KABOBS

1 1/2 pounds vension round steak
1/2 cup olive oil
1/2 cup pineapple juice
1/4 cup red wine vinegar
3 to 4 drops hot sauce
2 cloves garlic, minced
1/2 teaspoon basil
1/2 teaspoon oregano
1 teaspoon salt
1 large onion, quartered
1 pound medium-size fresh mushrooms
1 pound small-size cherry tomatoes
2 (8-ounce) cans pineapple chunks
12 (6-inch) wooden skewers, soaked in water overnight
vegetable cooking spray

1. Trim tallow from venison; cut venison into 1 to 1 1/2-inch cubes.
2. Place venison cubes in shallow dish; stir in olive oil, pineapple juice, red wine vinegar, hot sauce, garlic, basil, oregano and salt. Refrigerate 2-3 hours, turning occasionally.
3. Alternate venison cubes, onion sections, mushrooms, cherry tomatoes and pineapple chunks on wooden skewers; reserve marinade.
4. Spray grill rack with light coating of vegetable spray. Place skewered meat and vegetables on rack; grill over medium-hot coals 10 to 12 minutes or until meat reaches desired degree of doneness, turning and basting as needed with reserved marinade.

Makes 6 double servings.

The next time you get a craving, go to the freezer and dig out an elk or deer tenderloin and create the following dish.

CREAMED TENDERLOIN

2 tablespoons olive oil
1 large onion, diced
2 cloves garlic, minced
2 pounds venison tenderloins, cut into 4-inch lengths
1/2 cup water
1 (10 1/2-ounce) can cream of mushroom soup, undiluted
2 tablespoons flour
1 (4-ounce) can mushroom stems and pieces, drained
1/2 teaspoon salt
1/2 teaspoon black pepper, coarse ground
1/2 cup sour cream
4 cups hot cooked rice or noodles
Cayenne pepper

1. Heat olive oil in large skillet, add onion and garlic. Cook over medium heat until onions are crispy tender, set aside.
2. Add tenderloin pieces to same skillet; cook briefly over high heat, searing/browning both sides.
3. Reduce heat to low and simmer seared tenderloin 5 minutes; remove from heat and set aside, drain skillet.
4. Stir in water, cream of mushroom soup, flour, mushroom stems and pieces, salt and pepper; cook over medium heat, stirring constantly, until thickened.
5. Add seared tenderloins; simmer uncovered for 10 minutes.
6. Sir in sour cream, cover and simmer an additional 10 minutes.
7. Serve over hot cooked rice or noodles. Sprinkle to taste with cayenne pepper.

Makes 8 servings.

If you're a steak and pasta lover, the following combination is sure to please. Fresh venison only makes it that much better.

RED PEPPER STEAK

1 1/4 pound venison round, sirloin or sirloin tip steak
1/2 teaspoon salt
1/3 teaspoon cayenne pepper
1/2 teaspoon garlic powder
2 tablespoons olive oil
2 medium red bell peppers, stemed, seeded, cut into strips
4 green onions, chopped, including tops
1 beef bouillon cube
1/2 cup hot water
1 (14 1/2-ounce) can stewed tomatoes, undrained
4 to 5 drops hot sauce, optional
1/2 cup water
3 tablespoons beefy onion soup mix
4 cups hot cooked noodles

1. Trim/slice round steak (across grain) into 1/4-inch thick strips.
2. Combine steak strips, salt, cayenne pepper and garlic powder in mixing bowl; toss well and set aside.
3. Heat olive oil in large skillet; add red bell pepper strips, green onions and seasoned venison strips. Cook over medium heat to brown strips on all sides, stirring constantly; reduce heat to low.
4. Dissolve bouillon cube in 1/2 cup hot water; add to steak and red pepper mixture. Reduce heat; simmer 5 minutes.
5. Stir in stewed tomatoes, hot sauce, 1/2 cup water and beefy onion soup mix; simmer additional 5 minutes or until mixture thickens. Cover, and simmer 20 minutes or until steak reaches desired degree of doneness.
6. Serve over hot cooked noodles.

Makes 4 servings.

I was introduced to cubed steak and onions at an early age, and I've been been enjoying this scrumptious dish ever since.

CUBE STEAK AND ONIONS

1 1/2 pounds venison cube steaks
3/4 teaspoon salt
1/4 teaspoon cayenne pepper
1/4 teaspoon dried basil
1/4 teaspoon thyme
1/4 teaspoon garlic powder
1/2 cup flour
3 tablespoons olive oil
1 tablespoon red wine vinegar
1 tablespoon soy sauce
4 medium onions, sliced

1. Cut cube steaks into 1/2 to 3/4-inch-wide strips.
2. Combine salt, cayenne pepper, basil, thyme, garlic powder and flour; mix well.
3. Dredge steak strips in seasoned flour; set aside.
4. Heat olive oil in large skillet; add seasoned steak strips and cook over medium-high heat, stirring frequently to brown steaks on all sides. Drain; leave steaks in skillet.
5. Stir together red wine vinegar, soy sauce and water; add to skillet.
6. Add onion slices to skillet, cover, reduce heat and simmer 20 minutes or until steak reaches the desired degree of doneness.

Makes 6 servings.

If you're a steak lover, but too busy to spend much time in the kitchen, whip up a batch of fried finger steaks. They're easy to make and won't take a lot of time.

FRIED FINGER STEAKS

2 pounds venison top or bottom round steaks
1 teaspoon salt
1 teaspoon coriander, ground
1 teaspoon paprika
3 teaspoons lemon-pepper seasoning
2 eggs, beaten
1 cup buttermilk
1/2 cup Italian bread crumbs
1/4 cup olive oil

1. Cut venison steaks into finger-size strips; place strips in medium-size plastic bag.
2. Combine salt, coriander, paprika and lemon-pepper seasoning in small bowl; mix well. Sprinkle over steak strips; shake bag well.
3. Combine eggs and buttermilk in small bowl; mix well. Dredge seasoned finger steaks in egg/buttermilk mixture. Dredge in Italian bread crumbs; set aside.
4. Heat olive oil in large skillet; add seasoned/breaded finger steaks and fry over medium heat for 8 minutes, or until steaks reach desired degree of doneness, turning occasionally.

Makes 8 servings.

If you want to be adventuresome and try something different, you'll want to experiment with this proven favorite.

SIRLOIN TIP POCKETS

2 cups toasted bread crumbs
1 small onion, diced
1 small bell pepper, seeded, diced
1 stalk celery, diced
2 tablespoons fresh parsley, chopped
1/2 teaspoon sage
1/2 teaspoon thyme
1/2 teaspoon garlic salt
1 beef bouillon cube, diluted in 1 cup hot water
1 1/2 pounds venison sirloin tip steaks, 1/2-inch thick
1/4 cup flour
1/4 cup Italian bread crumbs
1/2 teaspoon salt
1/4 teaspoon black pepper, table grind
1 cup olive oil

1. Place bread crumbs, onion, bell pepper, celery, fresh parsley, sage, thyme and garlic salt in a medium-sized mixing bowl. Add bouillon broth mixture; toss well.

2. Top venison sirloin steaks evenly with stuffing mixture; fold over steaks and fasten together with toothpicks.

3. In a small bowl, combine flour, 1/2 teaspoon salt, Italian bread crumbs, and 1/4 teaspoon pepper; mix well. Gently dredge each stuffed steak seasoned flour mixture.

4. Heat olive oil in medium-size skillet. Add seasoned steak pockets, brown both sides and cook slowly over medium heat 15 minutes,turning occasionally.

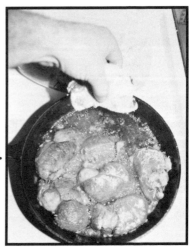

Query any outdoor cook about what gives his grilled steaks that unique flavor and you're likely to hear that it's his special barbecue sauce.

BBQ STEAK SANDWICHES

1/2 cup butter
1/2 cup minced onion
1/2 cup catsup
1/2 cup chili sauce
1/2 cup brown sugar, packed
4 tablespoons honey
3 tablespoons apple cider vinegar
1 tablespoon prepared mustard
2 tablespoons lemon juice
2 teaspoons Worcestershire sauce
1 teaspoon cayenne pepper
2 pounds venison round steaks, cut 1-inch thick
8 hamburger rolls, toasted

1. Combine butter, minced onion, catsup, chili sauce, brown
   sugar, honey, vinegar, mustard, lemon juice, Worcestershire sauce,
   and cayenne pepper in medium sauce pan; stir well.
2. Simmer barbecue sauce over medium-low heat 20 minutes, stirring
   frequently; remove from heat and set aside to cool.
3. Pour cooled barbecue sauce into shallow dish. Submerge steaks
   in mixture; refrigerate 6 to 8 hours, turning occasionally.
4. Next day, remove steaks from sauce; reserve sauce.
5. Grill steaks over medium-hot coals 8 to 10 minutes on each side,
   or until steaks reach desired degree of doneness.
6. Heat reserved barbecue sauce. Slice steaks (across grain) 1/8-
   inch thick; stir into cooked barbecue sauce.
7. Serve between toasted hamburger rolls.

Makes 8 servings.

If you're looking for a change of pace at mealtime, try this stir-fry recipe. It's simple to make and easy on the waistline.

TERIYAKI STEAK AND RICE

1 pound venison tenderloins or loins
2 tablespoons soy sauce
1 1/2 tablespoons olive oil
1 tablespoon red wine vinegar
1 tablespoon lemon juice
1 tablespoon brown sugar
1 tablespoon molasses
1/3 teaspoon dry mustard
1/2 teaspoon ground ginger
1 red bell pepper, seeded, sliced into 1/4-inch strips
1 green bell pepper, seeded, sliced into 1/4-inch strips
4 cups hot cooked rice

1. Slice tenderloins into thin (1/8-inch) strips; set aside.
2. Combine soy sauce, olive oil, red wine vinegar, lemon juice, brown sugar, molasses, dry mustard and ginger powder in a small mixing bowl; mix well.
3. Heat wok at medium-high heat (325 degrees) for 2 minutes. Stir in soy sauce mixture, bell pepper strips and tenderloin strips; stir-fry 4 to 5 minutes.
4. Reduce heat and slow-cook, uncovered, until steak mixture is steaming hot.
5. Serve over hot cooked rice.

Makes 4 servings.

The aroma of simmering apple cider and deer chops conjures up memories of Westfield, Pennsylvania, and the family farm where I grew up. This was one of Grandpa Cutlip's favorites.

APPLE CIDER CHOPS

1/4 cup flour
1/2 teaspoon dry mustard
1/2 teaspoon salt
1/4 teaspoon cayenne pepper
1/4 teaspoon allspice
1/4 teaspoon ground ginger
8 venison chops, cut 1-inch thick
1/4 cup olive oil
2 cups apple cider
2 tablespoons brown sugar
3 apples, peeled and quartered
1/3 cup raisins
1/4 cup currants, dried
1/3 teaspoon ground cinnamon
4 cups hot cooked rice

1. Combine flour, dry mustard, salt, cayenne pepper, allspice and ginger in small mixing bowl; mix well. Reserve left over flour.
2. Dredge venison chops in flour mixture. Heat olive oil in Dutch oven and cook dredged chops over medium-high heat until chops are browned on both sides; remove. Drain Dutch oven.
3. Stir in apple cider, brown sugar and reserved flour; cook over medium heat 2 minutes, stirring constantly until smooth. Remove from heat.
4. Place chops in cider mixture and top with apple quarters, raisins, currants and cinnamon. Cover and bake in preheated 350-degree oven for 1 hour or until chops are tender.
5. Serve over hot cooked rice.

Makes 4 double servings.

When it's time to plan the evening menu, choosing the main course is often the toughest decision to make. The next time you're stumped, try a skillet of glazed chops.

GLAZED ORANGE CHOPS

3 tablespoons olive oil
8 venison chops, cut 3/4-inch to 1-inch thick
1/4 cup orange juice
3/4 teaspoon salt
1/4 cup brown sugar, packed
1/4 cup corn syrup
1/2 cup orange juice
1 seedless orange, peeled, sectioned, rind grated
1 (11-ounce) can Mandarin orange sections, undrained
1 (16-ounce) can whole berry cranberry sauce
1 tablespoon lemon juice
4 cups hot cooked rice

1. Heat olive oil in large skillet, add venison chops and cook over medium-high heat, turning to brown chops on both sides; drain.
2. Add 1/4 cup orange juice and salt to skillet. Cover, and simmer over low heat for 1 hour; remove chops from skillet.
3. Stir in brown sugar, corn syrup, 1/2 cup orange juice, peeled orange sections, grated orange rind, Mandarin orange sections, cranberry sauce and lemon juice. Cook over medium-high heat 5 minutes, stirring constantly.
4. Return chops to skillet mixture; simmer 5 minutes.
5. Serve over hot-cooked rice.

Makes 4 double servings.

Grilling prime cuts of venison outdoors is fast becoming a favorite pastime for today's hunters, and nothing beats the flavor of marinated thick-cut steaks.

GRILLED ROUND

1 (3 to 4-pound) venison round steak, cut 2 inches thick
1/4 cup Italian dressing, oil based
2 tablespoons olive oil
2 tablespoons red wine vinegar
1 tablespoon granulated onions
2 tablespoons dehydrated bell peppers
1/2 teaspoon dried basil
1/2 teaspoon dried marjoram
1/2 teaspoon garlic powder

1. Pierce surface of both sides of venison round steak repeatedly with fork to tenderize.
2. Combine olive oil, red wine vinegar, Italian dressing, granulated onions, dehydrated bell pepper, basil, marjoram and garlic powder in shallow dish; mix well.
3. Add pierced steak to Italian dressing mixture, flipflop steak, then cover. Refrigerate overnight, turning steak occasionally.
4. Remove steak from marinade, reserving marinade. Grill steak over medium-hot coals for 15 to 20 minutes on each side, or until steak reaches desired degree of doneness, basting steak frequently with reserved marinade.

Makes 8 to 10 servings.

For a delicious meal that tastes great and can be prepared with relative ease, try the following recipe.

SWISS STEAK

3 tablespoons olive oil
3 pounds venison cube steaks
1 large onion, chopped
1 large bell pepper, chopped
1 (8 oounce) can mushroom stems & pieces, drained
1 cup hot water
1 (1.25 ounce) package beef soup mix
1/4 cup flour
1 cup milk
1/2 teaspoon salt
1/2 teaspoon black pepper, coarse ground
6 cups hot cooked noodles

1. Heat olive oil in electric frying pan. Add cube steaks and cook over medium heat until cube steaks are browned on both sides; set aside.
2. Add onion, bell pepper and mushroom stems and pieces to frying pan. Cook over medium heat, stirring frequently, until onions are crispy tender; drain.
3. Stir in hot water, beef soup mix, flour, milk, salt and pepper; simmer over low heat, stirring constantly, about 3 minutes, or until mixture is smooth and bubbly.
4. Submerge browned cube steaks into beef soup mixture, cover, and cook at 325 degrees for 1 to 1 1/2 hours or until cube steaks are fork tender.
5. Serve over hot cooked noodles.

Makes 6 servings.

I had my first encounter with steak & onions in the early 1960s. The late Blanche Harrison of Bath, New York, bless her heart, was the hostess and cook. Her venison steak & onions were absolutely delicious.

STEAK & ONIONS

1/2 cup flour
1/2 teaspoon salt
1/2 teaspoon black pepper, coarse ground
1/2 teaspoon garlic powder
4 tablespoons olive oil
1/1/2 pounds venison round steaks, cut 1/2-inch thick
6 medium onions, sliced
1 (8-ounce) can mushroom stems and pieces, drained
1 (10 1/2-ounce) can cream of onion soup, undiluted
1 (10 1/2-ounce) can cream of mushroom soup, undiluted
1 soup can of water
6 cups hot cooked noodles
Parmesan cheese

1. Combine flour, salt, pepper and garlic powder in small lunch bag; shake well.
2. Heat olive oil in Dutch oven; add seasoned steaks and cook over medium-high heat until steaks are browned on both sides. Set browned steaks aside.
3. Add onions and mushrooms to pan drippings and cook over medium heat until onions are crispy tender, stirring frequently; drain Dutch oven.
4. Stir in mushroom stems and pieces, cream of onion soup, cream of mushroom soup, water and browned steaks; simmer 1 1/2 hours, or until steaks are fork tender.
5. Serve with hot cooked noodles; top each serving with sprinkling of Parmesan cheese.

Makes 6 servings.

Surprise the hunters in your family with a home-cooked meal featuring venison Steak Burgundy as the main course.

STEAK BURGUNDY

2 1/2 pounds venison sirloin tip steaks, 3/4-inch thick
1 teaspoon salt
1/2 teaspoon black pepper, table grind
8 strips bacon, fried and crumbled
3 beef bouillon cubes, crushed
3 cups hot water
1/2 cup red Burgundy
2 cloves garlic, minced
2 medium onions, quartered
6 medium carrots, quartered
1 small head cabbage, quartered
1 (8-ounce) can mushroom stems and pieces
2 tablespoons flour
6 cups hot cooked noodles

1. Pound or cube venison steaks; season with salt and pepper.
2. Cook bacon in Dutch oven over medium heat until bacon is crispy and crumbles easily.
3. Cook seasoned steaks in bacon drippings over medium-high heat, turning frequently, until steaks are browned on both sides; drain excess bacon grease.
4. Reduce heat. Stir in bouillon cubes, water, Burgundy and garlic, cover; simmer 1 hour.
5. Add onions, carrots, cabbage and mushroom stems and pieces. Cover; simmer 1/2 hour, or until carrots are nearly tender. (Note: you may add additional water if necessary.)
6. Stir in flour; simmer, uncovered, until thickened and bubbly, stirring constantly.
7. Serve over hot cooked noodles.

Makes 6 servings.

HOW TO ROLL AND TIE A ROAST

Venison roasts cut from the neck, shoulder or hind quarter have excellent flavor. Neck and shoulder roasts are the best when prepared as *pot* roasts. The hind-quarter cuts, such as the rump, round, sirloin, and sirloin tip, are usually better when prepared as *oven* roasts.

OVEN ROASTS: For the best venison oven roast, sear the outside quickly at 500 degrees and then slow roast at 325 to 350 degrees until the internal temperature reaches a 130 to 135-degree perfection, medium and pink in the middle.

POT ROASTS: Pot roasts are usually browned on the outside in hot oil and then simmered to tender perfection in liquid. Later, when the meat is near fork tender, vegetables, such as potatoes, carrots, cabbage, etc. may be added.

Bone-in roasts are delicious, and there's little doubt the bone adds overall flavor to the roast. But if you've tried to carve a bone-in shoulder or neck roast, you know the difficulty involved in trying to remove the meat from the bone. It's often embarassing and downright aggravating if you get stuck with the carving detail.   There's a better way. Iimpress dinner guests with a succulent, rolled and tied venison roast. The process is simple.

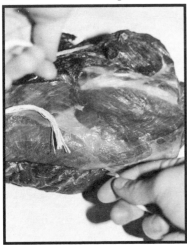

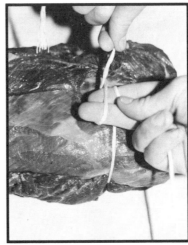

1. Begin by picking up the loose end of the butcher twine with your left hand. Use your right hand to pull the twine under the roast as shown above.

2. Using the photo as a guide, use your left hand to make a loop around your index and middle finger.

HOW TO ROLL AND TIE A ROAST

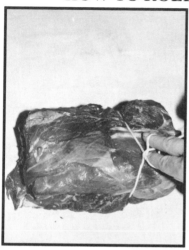

3. Twist your right hand to the right so that your middle finger is above your index finger.

4. Use your middle finger to pull the loose string (twine) through the loop

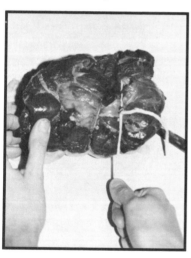

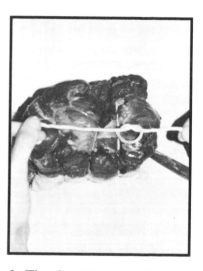

5. Pull the main string (twine) downward. Grasp the roast with your left hand, then using your right, give the twine a quick jerk, locking the knot.

6. Tie a knot to secure the lock. Cut off the ends and repeat the procedure the length of the roast. Cut the roast to size, double wrap and freeze.

Can't get enough barbecue? Then try this savory recipe. It's easy to make and nearly melts in your mouth.

BARBECUE ROAST

2 tablespoons olive oil
4 pounds venison shoulder roast, boneless, rolled
1 cup catsup
1 cup hickory smoke barbecue sauce
1 cup water
2 tablespoons red wine vinegar
2 tablespoons Worcestershire sauce
2 tablespoons brown sugar, packed
2 tablespoons minced onion
1 teaspoon garlic powder
1 teaspoon chili powder
1 teaspoon salt
8 medium potatoes, unpeeled, quartered

1. Heat olive oil in Dutch oven; add venison shoulder roast. Cook over medium-high heat, turning as needed to brown roast on all sides; drain.
2. Mix together catsup, barbecue sauce, water, red wine vinegar, Worcestershire sauce, brown sugar, minced onion, garlic powder, chili powder and salt.
3. Pour mixture over browned roast, cover and bake in preheated 350-degree oven for 4 to 5 hours or until roast is nearly fork tender.
4. Place potato quarters around roast and bake an additional 30 minutes or until potatoes are tender.

Makes 6 to 8 servings.

Whether you're a novice or experienced cook, you'll get excellent results with the following recipe. Add new potatoes and fresh-picked corn, and you'll have the makings for a great meal.

PEPPERED POT ROAST

1 1/2 teaspoon garlic salt
2 tablespoons peppercorns, 1/4 cracked
4 tablespoons flour
3 tablespoons olive oil
5 pound venison shoulder or neck roast, boneless
2 cups water
1 cup dry red wine
2 bouillon cubes, crushed
2 tablespoons granulated onion
2 tablespoons brown sugar, packed
1 teaspoon coriander, ground
2 tablespoons flour
1/4 cup water

1. Mix together garlic salt, cracked peppercorns and flour in medium-size bowl; dredge roast in mixture, using all of the seasoned flour.
2. Heat olive oil in Dutch oven; add seasoned roast and cook over medium-high heat until roast is brown on all sides, remove roast, set aside.
3. Stir in water, wine, bouillon cubes, granulated onion, brown sugar and coriander; simmer 3 minutes, stirring frequently.
4. Add browned roast, cover, and simmer 2 1/2 to 3 hours or until roast is fork tender.
5. To make gravy: Set roast aside. Stir flour and water into pan drippings; cook over medium heat, stirring constantly, until gravy is smooth and bubbly. Add more water if necessary.

Makes 8 servings.

When you're having friends over for dinner, nothing is more impressive than a properly prepared Prime Rib of Venison.

PRIME RIB OF VENISON

2 beef bouillon cubes
2 tablespoons beef soup mix
3 cups hot water
1 large onion, chopped
6 to 7 pound venison standing-rib roast
salt
garlic pepper
spiced crab apples
fresh parsley sprigs

1. Dissolve bouillon cubes and beef soup mix in 3 cups hot water, add chopped onion and stir well. Pour into baking dish.
2. Sprinkle sides and back of venison prime rib with salt and garlic pepper (to taste).
3. Insert meat thermometer into the thickest portion of the roast. Place roast in preheated 400-degree oven; cook, uncovered, 30 minutes or until well browned.
4. Baste with onion/soup stock; reduce heat to 325 degrees. Bake, uncovered for 1 1/2 hours or until meat thermometer reaches 155 to 160 degrees, basting often with onion/soup stock.
5. Slice between each rib. Serve with small bowl of stock; garnish with spiced crab apples and parsley twigs.

1. Dissolve bouillon cubes and beef soup mix in 3 cups hot water, add chopped onion, stir and pour into baking dish.

2. Sprinkle sides and back of vension prime rib (to taste) with salt and garlic pepper.

3. Insert meat thermometer into the thickest portion of roast. Place roast in preheated 400-dgree oven; cook, uncovered, 30 minutes or until well browned.

4. Baste with onion/soup stock. Reduce heat to 325 degrees and bake, uncovered, 1 1/2 hours, or until meat thermometer reaches 155-160 degrees, basting often with onion/ soup stock.

When the end of summer's nearing garden-fresh vegetables abound, thaw out a venison shoulder roast and put together the following recipe.

POT ROAST AND VEGETABLES

Salt
Garlic pepper
4 pounds venison shoulder roast, boneless
2 tablespoons olive oil
2 beef bouillon cubes
2 cups hot water
2 medium onions, quartered
4 tablespoons flour
2/3 cup water
10 to 12 small potatoes
6 medium carrots, cut into 1-inch pieces
1 small cabbage, quartered
2 cups cut green beans

1. Season roast to taste with salt and garlic pepper.
2. Heat olive oil in dutch oven. Cook seasoned roast over medium-high heat until browned on all sides; pour off drippings.
3. Dissolve bouillon cubes in 2 cups hot water.
4. Arrange onions around roast; pour bouillon stock over roast. Cover; simmer 3 hours or until meat is nearly fork tender.
5. Remove meat from Dutch oven; cover to keep warm.
6. Blend flour and 2/3 cup water together; slowly stir mixture into stock. Cook over medium heat until mixture is smooth, stirring constantly.
7. Replace roast; arrange potatoes, carrots, cabbage and green beans around roast and cook 30 minutes longer or until vegetables are crispy tender.

Makes 8 servings.

There are probably as many different venison roast recipes as hunters. Roast Burgundy competes with best of the recipes. Its savory, mouth-watering flavor is sure to please.

ROAST BURGUNDY

1 1/2 cups Burgundy
1/2 teaspoon basil
1/2 teaspoon thyme, ground
1/2 teaspoon salt
1/4 teaspoon black pepper, table grind
2 beef bouillon cubes, crushed
2 tablespoons olive oil
4 to 5 pound venison round or sirloin tip roast
1 medium onion, chopped
4 carrots, sliced thick
1/3 cup butter, melted
1/3 cup flour
1 (8-ounce) can mushroom stems and pieces

1. Combine Burgundy, basil, thyme, salt, pepper and bouillon cubes in deep bowl; stir well.
2. Place roast in Burgundy mixture, turning 2 or 3 times; marinate in refrigerator overnight, turning ocassionally.
3. Remove roast, reserving marinade.
4. Heat olive oil in Dutch oven; add roast and onion. Cook over medium-high heat, turning as needed to brown roast on all sides.
5. Pour reserved marinade over roast; cover. Reduce heat; simmer 1 1/4 hour or until roast nearly reaches the desired degree of doneness (internal temperature of 135 degrees).
6. Add carrots and simmer until carrots are crispy tender. Remove roast and carrots to serving platter; cover.
7. Combine butter, flour and mushroom stems and pieces in ample-sized bowl; stir well until smooth. Stir into Burgundy mixture; cook over medium heat, stirring constantly, until thickened and bubbly. Serve with roast.

Makes 8 to 10 servings.

If you're fond of deli-style roast beef sandwiches, then you need to try this recipe. The rich flavor of venison makes a delicious deli-style sandwich filling. You won't be able to eat just one!

DELI-STYLE MEAT

1 1/2 teaspoons garlic powder
1 1/2 teaspoons onion powder
3 teaspoons yellow mustard seeds, ground
1/4 cup Worcestershire sauce
1/4 cup lemon juice
2 tablespoons prepared horseradish
1 cup dry red wine
1 (8-ounce) can tomato sauce
4 pound venison top round roast

1. Combine garlic powder, onion powder, ground mustard, Worcestershire sauce, lemon juice, horseradish, red wine and tomato sauce in a deep roasting dish; stir well.
2. Place venison roast in marinade mixture, turning 2 or 3 times. Marinate in refrigerator overnight, turning occasionally.
3. Drain marinade from roast, discard.
4. Lift up roast, position rack in baking dish, replace roast and insert meat thermometer into thickest portion of roast. Bake about 1 1/2 hours at 350-degrees, or until meat thermometer reaches 140 degrees (rare) or 150 degrees (medium-rare).
5. Remove roast from oven, cool 3 minutes, wrap tightly with quality plastic wrap and refrigerate overnight.
6. Next day, slice thinly.

Makes about 3 pounds of deli-style roast venison.

If you're a '90s gal and would rather be hunting than slaving in the kitchen, this might be the Sauerbraten recipe for you.

SAUERBRATEN

2 cups water
1/4 cup brown sugar
1 cup red wine
2 tablespoons pickling spice
1 large onion, thin sliced
1 1/2 teaspoons salt
1 tablespoon black pepper, 1/4 grind
2 pound venison top round roast
2 tablespoons olive oil
1/4 cup cottage cheese
1/4 cup sour cream
1/2 cup gingersnap cookies, crumbled

1. Combine water, brown sugar, red wine, pickling spice, onions salt and black pepper in large glass bowl; stir well. Reserve 1 cup brown sugar/Burgundy marinade mixture in refrigerator.
2. Submerge venison top round roast in remaining marinade, turning 2 or 3 times. Cover and refrigerate overnight.
3. Next day, remove roast from marinade.
4. Heat olive oil in Dutch oven, add venison top round roast. Cook over medium-high heat, turning as needed to brown roast on all sides; drain.
5. Pour marinade over roast. Bring mixture to a boil, cover and reduce heat. Simmer 45 to 50 minutes or until venison is tender; drain Dutch oven.
6. Remove roast and cut into 1/8-inch thick slices; cover.
7. To make Sauerbraten sauce, combine 1 cup reserved marinade, cottage cheese, sour cream and gingersnap cookies in Dutch oven; cook over medium heat, stirring constantly until heated through.
8. Serve roast with Sauerbraten sauce.

Makes 8 servings.

By using the crockpot and planning ahead, you can fish your favorite stretch of river in the morning and still enjoy a hot venison sandwich when you return home.

CROCKPOT ROAST

2 tablespoons olive oil
1 small onion, diced
2 gloves garlic, minced
5-pound venison sirloin tip or shoulder roast, boneless
1/4 cup butter
1 cup catsup
1/3 cup brown sugar, packed
1 1/2 tablespoons apple cider vinegar
1 tablespoon Worcestershire sauce
1 teaspoon salt
1 teaspoon mustard powder
2 loaves garlic bread, halved, lightly toasted, then quartered

1. Heat olive oil in skillet; add onions and garlic. Cook over medium heat until onions are crispy tender.
2. Set onion mixture aside, add roast. Cook over medium-high heat, turning as needed to brown roast on all sides. Set roast aside.
3. To make onion sauce: combine onion mixture, butter, catsup, brown sugar, vinegar, Worcestershire sauce, salt and mustard powder in crockpot, stir well. Turn crockpot to "simmer" setting.
4. Submerge browned roast in onion sauce, turning 2 or 3 times. Cover; simmer 6 to 8 hours or until roast is fork tender.
5. Crumble roast; mix with onion sauce and serve between quarters of toasted garlic bread.

Makes 8 servings.

I enjoyed my first haunch of venison at a summer outing in Canadice, New York. Long-time friend, Lynn Gorton, prepared the memorable meal. The meat was mouth-wateringly delicious.

HAUNCH OF VENISON

1/2 cup water
2 cups soy sauce
1 1/2 cup vegetable oil
1/2 cup red wine vinegar
3 teaspoons salt
2 teaspoons garlic granules
2 tablespoons black pepper, coarse ground
8 to 10-pound venison haunch, boneless, rolled and tied
Meat pump or syringe
Garlic pepper
Seasoning salt

1. To make marinade, combine water, soy sauce, vegetable oil, red wine vinegar, salt, garlic granules and pepper in 2-quart jar; shake vigorously until mixed well.
2. Place venison haunch in large, non-metallic vessel. Fill meat pump with marinade. Pump venison to 10% of its own weight.
3. Pour remaining marinade over venison, turning 2 or 3 times. Marinate venison in refrigerator 24 hours, turning occasionally.
4. Remove roast from marinade; sprinkle to taste with garlic pepper and seasoning salt.
5. Position haunch on spit; cook over medium-hot coals (350 to 400 degrees) for about 5 hours or until venison reaches the desired degree of doneness.
6. Check correct doneness with meat thermometer; 140 degrees for rare, 150 degrees for medium rare and 160 degrees for medium.
7. To serve, slice while hot according to individual instructions.

   Feeds group of 30 to 40 people.

There's nothing like a hearty stew to warm your bones after a long day afield.

CHUNKY STEW

2 tablespoons olive oil
2 pounds venison stew meat, cut into 1-2-inch cubes
2 cups water
2 beef bouillon cubes
1/2 teaspoon salt
1/2 teaspoon black pepper, table grind
1/2 teaspoon garlic powder
1 medium onion, quartered
4 carrots, quartered
4 medium potatoes, quartered
1 small head cabbage, quartered
2 stalks celery, chopped
1 (16-ounce) can whole kernel corn
1 (15-ounce) can butter beans
3 cups water
1 loaf garlic bread, warmed and lightly toasted

1. Heat olive oil in Dutch oven, add venison stew meat and cook over medium-high heat, stirring as needed until venison is browned on all sides. Drain.
2. Stir in 2 cups water, bouillon cubes, salt, pepper and garlic powder. Cover and simmer 2 hours, or until meat is tender.
3. Add onion, carrots, potatoes, cabbage, celery, corn, butter beans and 3 cups water. Cover and simmer 30 to 40 minutes, or until cabbage is crispy tender.
4. Serve hot with lightly toasted garlic bread.

Makes 8 man-size servings.

The following recipe is a cinch, even for reluctant camp cooks. Simply cook the meat according to instructions then add the canned vegetables and sour cream. Excellent!

CAMP STEW

2 tablespoons olive oil
2 large onion, chopped
2 pounds venison stew meat
2 teaspoons salt
1/2 teaspoon black pepper, table grind
1 teaspoon garlic powder
2 teaspoons basil
1/4 cup brown sugar
2 (8-ounce) cans tomato sauce
2 (16-ounce) cans whole kernel corn
1 (16-ounce) can peas
1 (16-ounce) can green beans
3 (16-ounce) cans sliced potatoes
1 (16-ounce) carton sour cream

1. Heat olive oil in 14-inch Dutch oven. Add onion and venison stew meat; cook over medium-high heat, stirring as needed to brown venison on all sides.
2. Stir in salt, pepper, garlic powder, basil, brown sugar and tomato sauce. Cover, reduce heat and simmer 2 to 3 hours or until meat is near fork tender.
3. Add whole kernel corn, peas, green beans and potatoes. Cover and cook over medium heat until potatoes are cooked through.
4. Stir in sour cream, cover. Reduce heat; simmer 5 minutes.
5. Serve while hot with fresh bakery rolls.

Makes 8 to 10 servings.

The fall harvest means an abundance of fresh-picked vegetables including cabbage, carrots, potatoes and onions. So why not use these healthy treats into a hearty venison stew?

STEAK & ONION STEW

2 pounds venison shoulder steak
2 tablespoons olive oil
1 1/4 cup apple cider
1 1/4 cup water
1 (1.25-ounce) package beefy onion soup mix
1 (10 3/4-ounce) can tomato soup, undiluted
2 tablespoons red wine vinegar
2 tablespoons brown sugar
1 teaspoon garlic powder
1/2 teaspoon cumin
1/2 teaspoon salt
1/2 teaspoon black pepper, table grind
1 pound carrots, cut into 1-inch slices
1 pound potatoes, cut into 1-inch cubes
1 pound cabbage, chopped
2 medium onions, chopped

1. Cut venison shoulder steaks into 1/2 to 1-inch cubes. Brown both sides in Dutch oven in hot olive oil, drain.
2. Stir in apple cider, water, beefy onion soup mix, tomato soup, red wine vinegar, brown sugar, garlic powder, cumin, salt and pepper. Bring to a boil, cover, reduce heat and simmer 1 hour.
3. Add carrots, potatoes, cabbage and chopped onions; cover and simmer additional 20 to 25 minutes or until vegetables are crispy tender.

Makes 8 servings.

Want to impress your grandmother this holiday season. Show up at Thanksgiving or Christmas with a fresh-baked venison mincemeat pie. You're bound to get a holiday hug!

MINCEMEAT

4 pounds venison stew meat, diced
1 pound beef suet
6 tart apples, peeled and chopped
1 1/2 pounds seedless raisins
1 pound dried currants
4 cups brown sugar
1 tablespoon salt
1 teaspoon ground cloves
1 1/4 teaspoons allspice
1 tablespoon ground cinnamon
1/2 cup apple cider vinegar
1/2 cup molasses
1 quart apple cider

1. Double check to make sure you have all the ingredients on hand. Simmer stew meat in a large, heavy kettle until stew meat is tender. Set meat aside to cool; reserve stock.

MINCEMEAT

2. Cool cooked meat and beef suet. Grind through the coarse plate of a meat grinder/food chopper one time. Place meat and fat into heavy kettle.

3. Stir in apples, raisins, currants, brown sugar, salt, cloves, allspice, cinnamon, vinegar, molasses, apple cider and reserved stock.

4. Simmer mincemeat mixture for 1 hour, stirring frequently.

5. Pack mincemeat in sterilized jars, leaving at least 1-inch head room; process at 10 lbs. pressure for 20 minutes (following pressure cooker manufacturer instructions).

My favorite marinades are a combination of acidic liquids and distinctive seasonings which help tenderize the meat while imparting specific flavors to wild game.

GARLIC MARINADE

1/2 cup olive oil
1/2 cup red wine vinegar
2 teaspoons garlic granules
1 tablespoon basil
1/8 teaspoon salt
1/4 teaspoon white pepper

TERIYAKI MARINADE

2 tablespoons olive oil
1 tablespoon lemon juice
1 teaspoon Worcestershire sauce
1/2 cup soy sauce
1/4 cup brown sugar, packed
1/3 teaspoon ginger, ground
1/4 teaspoon garlic granules

MEXICAN MARINADE

1/3 cup olive oil
1/3 cup lime juice
2 tablespoons tequila
1/2 teaspoon jalapeno powder
1/2 teaspoon garlic granules
1 tablespoon dried cilantro
1/8 teaspoon salt

TANGY HERB MARINADE

1/2 cup olive oil
1/4 cup red wine vinegar
2 teaspoons prepared horseradish
2 tablespoons minced onion
1 teaspoon dried mustard
1 teaspoon oregano
1 teaspoon basil
1/8 teaspoon salt
1/2 teaspoon cayenne pepper

SWEET & SOUR MARINADE

1/3 cup olive oil
1/3 cup apple cider vinegar
1/3 cup brown sugar, packed
1/2 teaspoon dried mustard
1/2 teaspoon coriander, ground
1/8 teaspoon salt

SALAD DRESSING MARINADES

Marinade 1 pound of venison in 1/2 cup of your favorite salad dressing. Italian, French, Russian, Catalina, Red Wine Vinegar, etc. have worked well for me.

MARINADE USAGE: 1. Combine all ingredients for particular marinade in mixing bowl; mix well.   2. Place 1 to 3 pounds of venison steaks in shallow roasting dish; pour marinade mixture over steaks and refrigerate 3 to 4 hours, turning occasionally.   3. Bake, broil or grill in usual manner until steaks reach the desired degree of doneness.

Want a neat breakfast idea? The following recipes take little time and effort and turn out nearly perfect every time.

BAKED HASH (CORNED MEAT)

3 cups cooked corned venison, chopped
1 1/2 cups cooked potatoes, mashed with skins on
1 large onion, diced, fryed to crispy tender
1 1/2 cups milk
3/4 cup Italian bread crumbs
6 large eggs

1. Combine corned venison, mashed potatoes, cooked onion, milk, and Italian bread crumbs in mixing bowl; mix well.
2. Place hash mixture in greased, square baking dish; bake in pre-heated 350-degree oven for 25 minutes. Remove from oven, break eggs over hash mixture and return to oven. Bake an additional 2 minutes, or until eggs reach desired degree of oneness.

COUNTRY HASH (ROAST VENISON)

2 tablespoons olive oil
1 medium onion, diced
3 cups left over venison roast, chopped
4 to 5 medium potatoes, diced
1/2 teaspoon salt
1/4 teaspoon black pepper, table grind
1 1/2 cups milk
3/4 cup Italian bread crumbs
6 large eggs

1. Heat olive oil in large skillet; add onion, venison roast, potatoes, salt and pepper. Cook, uncovered, over medium heat 20 minutes, turning frequently, until potatoes are cooked through. Drain.
2. Reduce heat, break eggs over hash mixture; cover. Cook addi tional 2 to 3 minutes or until eggs reach desired degree of doneness.

Both recipes makes 6 servings.

Whether your cooking at home or at hunting camp, this recipe is sure to please.

BROCCOLI STEAK FRY

1/3 cup olive oil
1/2 cup apple cider vinegar
1/2 cup sugar
1/2 teaspoon ginger
1/2 teaspoon celery seed, whole
1 teaspoon minced onion
1 teaspoon salt
1/2 teaspoon black pepper, 1/4 ground
2 bunches broccoli
1 1/2 pounds venison round steak
3 tablespoons cornstarch
3 tablespoons water
3 tablespoons soy sauce
6 cups hot cooked rice

1. To make marinade: combine olive oil, vinegar, sugar, ground ginger, celery seed, minced onion, salt and pepper in glass or plastic mixing bowl; stir well.
2. Cut off and discard tough portion of broccoli stems. Break off individual flowerets. Place flowerets in marinade; toss well.
3. Cut venison round steak into 1/8-inch strips. Place strips in marinade; toss well. Refrigerate 4 hours, tossing occasionally.
4. Pour broccoli/steak mixture into large skillet or wok. Stir in cornstarch,water and soy sauce; stir fry over medium-high heat 8 minutes.
5. Serve over hot cooked rice.

Makes 6 servings.

Properly prepared venison makes the best product. And because the canning process tenderizes even the toughest cuts, clean, lean trim from the neck, shank and shoulder can be used for canned venison.

CANNED VENISON

20 pounds fresh-cut venison
Salt or Seasoning Salt

1. Remove hairs and foreign matter from the venison.
2. Cut away bloodshot, tallow and the thickest gristle from venison cut into 1" to 2" cubes, (Need 14 pounds venison cubes).
3. Check jar mouths for nicks and cracks. Wash jars in hot, soapy water; rinse well. Cover jars with clean hot water; leave covered with hot water until ready to use.
4. Pack venison into hot jars, pressing down firmly to get as much venison into each jar as possible (roughly 2 pounds per jar), leaving 1-inch headspace from the top of each jar.
5. Add 1/2 to 1 teaspoon salt or seasoning salt to each jar.
6. Wipe the top and threads of each jar with clean, damp cloth.
7. Screw on lid covers according to manufacturer instructions.
8. Place each filled jar on rack in steam-pressure cooker; fill pressure cooker canner according to manufacturer instructions.
9. Fasten pressure canner lid securely according to manufacturer instructions.
10. Open petcock; cook over medium-high heat 10 minutes or until steam intensifies. Close Petcock and bring pressure back to 10 pounds pressure, or according to manufacturer instructions.
11. Process venison quarts 90 minutes at 10 pounds pressure according to manufacturer instructions.
12. Remove pressure canner from heat; allow pressure to fall to zero, wait 4 minutes, slowly remove petcock.
13. Unfasten cover; remove by tilting cover away from you so steam can escape safely. Remove jars; place on cloth a few inches apart. Twelve hours later, test jar seals according to manufacturer instructions. Store jars in dark, dry, cool place.
14. Refrigerate unsealed jars and consume within 1 week. Completely sealed jars should last up to 1 year.

Yields 7 quarts canned venison.

Nothing compares with the flavor of venison liver. And it's not nearly as fatty as its beef counterpart. Try this recipe and you'll see what I mean.

LIVER & ONIONS ITALIANO

Venison liver, soaked overnight in fresh, cold water
1/2 cup olive oil
3 medium bell peppers, seeded, chopped
4 medium onions, chopped
1/2 cup flour
2/3 teaspoon garlic salt
2/3 teaspoon garlic pepper
2 (8-ounce) cans tomato sauce
2 teaspoons Italian seasoning
Parmesan cheese

1. Drain venison liver, skin and cut into 1/2-inch slices. Reserve 2 pounds sliced liver.
2. Heat olive oil in large skillet. Add bell peppers and onions; cook over medium-high heat, stirring frequently, until onions are crispy tender, remove bell peppers and onions. Set aside.
3. Combine flour, garlic salt and garlic pepper in large mixing bowl; mix well. Dredge reserved liver slices in flour mixture.
4. Add dredged liver to skillet; cook over medium-high heat, turning as needed, until liver is browned on both sides. Drain.
5. Add tomato sauce, Italian seasoning, reserved bell pepper and onion; cover, reduce heat, simmer 10 to 15 minutes, or until liver reaches desired degree of doneness.
6. Sprinkle each serving with Parmesan cheese.

Makes 8 servings.

Some people hate liver. Others can't get enough. True enthusiasts should love this recipe since it brings out the best flavor qualities of venison liver.

BARBECUED LIVER

1/4 cup flour
1/4 teaspoon ginger
3/4 teaspoon salt
1/2 teaspoon white pepper
1 pound venison liver, skinned, sliced 1/2-inch thick
2 tablespoons olive oil
2 tablespoons butter
1/4 cup catsup
1/2 cup water
1 tablespoon red wine vinegar
1 tablespoon Worcestershire sauce
2 tablespoons brown sugar, packed
3 tablespoons minced onion

1. Combine flour, ginger, salt and white pepper in mixing bowl; mix well. Dredge liver slices in flour mixture.
2. Heat olive oil in large, heavy skillet; add dredged liver and cook over medium-high heat 10 minutes, turning as needed, until liver is browned on both sides, reduce heat.
3. Combine butter, catsup, water, red wine vinegar, Worcestershire sauce, brown sugar and minced onion in small sauce pan; stir well and cook over medium heat 5 minutes, stirring frequently.
4. Pour sauce over browned liver, cover, simmer 20 minutes or until liver reaches desired degree of doneness.

Makes 4 servings.

Looking for a great way to use your freshly canned venison (see page 53), then try the following recipe.

CHIMACHANGAS

2 tablespoons olive oil
2 pounds canned venison, shredded (see page 53)
2 cups chili sauce
1/2 cup catsup
6 to 8 drops hot sauce
2 teaspoons dried oregano
1 teaspoon cumin
1 teaspoon garlic granules
Processed cheese
6 (10-inch) flour tortillas

Taco sauce

1. Heat olive oil in large skillet, stir in shredded venison; cook over medium heat 5 minutes, stirring frequently to keep venison from burning reduce heat.
2. Stir in chili sauce, catsup, hot sauce, oregano, cumin and garlic granules; simmer, uncovered, 10 minutes, stirring as needed. Remove from heat, stir in processed cheese.
3. Place tortillas in covered baking dish; bake in preheated 350-degree oven four 15 minutes.
4. Divide venison mixture into sixths; place 1/6 of mixture in the middle of each tortilla, fold in the ends to partially enclose mixture, fold up bottom edge, roll up and pin together with tooth picks.
5. Carefully place 2 filled tortillas in hot oil; cook about 1 minute on each side or until tortillas are golden brown, remove from heat and place on double layer of paper towels in baking dish, cover to keep warm. Repeat cooking procedure with remain ing filled tortillas.
6. Serve with your favorite taco sauce.

Makes 6 servings.

You don't always have to spend your day slaving in the kitchen. This meal is easy and goes great with a garden salad.

MASHED POTATO/MEAT PIE

8 medium potatoes
2 eggs, beaten
1 cup milk
1/2 teaspoon basil
2 tablespoons olive oil
2 pounds venison round or sirloin tip steak, diced
1 medium onion, diced
1 teaspoon salt
1 teaspoon black pepper, 1/4 grind (coarse)
3 carrots, diced
2 (10 1/2-ounce) cans cream of mushroom soup
2 cups Monterey Jack cheese, grated

1. Boil potatoes with skins on until cooked through; drain.
2. Add eggs, milk and basil to cooked potatoes; mash, cover, and
   set aside.
3. Heat olive oil in medium skillet; add diced venison, onion, salt,
   pepper and carrots. Cook over medium-high heat, uncovered, 10
   minutes, stirring frequently to brown/cook all sides of meat.
4. Add cream of mushroom soup to meat mixture; mix well.
5. Spread meat mixture evenly in large baking dish. Top with
   mashed potatoes. Sprinkle with cheese. Bake in preheated 350-
   degree oven 40 minutes, or until cheese is golden brown.
6. Slice into 8 servings and serve with fresh garden salad.

Makes 8 servings.

It's easy to make and tastes great! What more could you ask for in a camp dish? You won't have a bunch of dirty dishes to wash and you'll impress your hunting buddies.

DUTCH OVEN BEANS

3 tablespoons olive oil
3 pounds venison stew meat, diced
2 large onions, chopped
2 bell peppers, chopped
2 (8-ounce) cans mushroom stems and pieces, drained
1 (8-ounce) can tomato sauce
1 (6-ounce) can tomato paste
7 to 8 drops hot sauce, or to taste
2 (28-ounce) cans pork and beans
1 (15-ounce) can butter beans
1/2 cup brown sugar, packed
2 tablespoons molasses
1 tablespoon ground mustard
2 teaspoons salt
1 teaspoon black pepper, table grind

1. Heat olive oil in Dutch oven, add diced venison stew meat, onions, bell peppers and mushroom stems and pieces; cook over medium-high heat, stirring often, until meat is browned, drain.
2. Reduce heat, stir in tomato sauce, tomato paste, hot sauce, pork and beans, butter beans, brown sugar, molasses, ground mustard, salt and pepper; cover, simmer 2 hours over hot coals, or until venison is fork tender, stirring occasionally.
3. Serve with big slices of French bread.

Makes 12 to 14 servings.

Experts say there's a knack to cooking wild game. However, putting together a venison foil bake is easy and the results are incredibly good!

FOIL BAKE

Aluminum foil (18-inch width)
4 (1/2-pound) venison round or loin steaks, cut 3/4-inch thick
4 slices bacon, uncooked, halved
4 carrots, quartered lengthwise
4 medium potatoes, quartered
4 medium onions, quartered
4 ears corn, shucked, halved
2 stalks celery, chopped fine
1/2 cup brown sugar, packed
1 1/2 teaspoon garlic powder
1/3 teaspoon basil
1/3 teaspoon marjoram, cut
1/24 teaspoon cayenne pepper
1 1/2 teaspoon salt

1. Tear off 4 (18" X 18") sheets heavy-duty aluminum foil; spread sheets out on counter.
2. Place venison steak in center of each foil, surround each with equal amount of carrots, potatoes, onions, celery and corn. Top each steak with 2 halves of bacon.
3. Combine brown sugar, garlic powder, basil, marjoram, pepper and salt in small shaker; shake well.
4. Sprinkle steaks and vegetables evenly with seasoned mixture.
5. Fold the edges of each square of aluminum foil together tightly so that steam can't escape, but be sure to make a pouch with ample air space.
6. Lay pouches on hot coals for 20 to 30 minutes, or until meat and vegetables reach desired degree of doneness.

Makes 4 servings.

Ever have one of those days when you're craving something different for supper? Give this recipe a try.

CROSSCUT SHANKS

1/4 cup flour
1 1/4 teaspoon salt
1/2 teaspoon pepper
2 pounds venison crosscut shanks, cut 1-inch thick
2 tablespoons olive oil
2 cups apple cider, divided
4 medium carrots, cut into 2-inch chunks
1 bunch broccoli, tough stem removed, cut into 1-inch pieces
8 small red potatoes, whole
2 tablespoons brown sugar, packed

1. To cut venison crosscuts, lay the hind shank on a cutting board, grasp the end of the shank with your free hand and simply cut 1-inch slices with a meat saw.
2. Combine flour, salt and pepper in plastic bag. Add crosscut shanks; shake well. Remove shanks.
3. Heat olive oil in Dutch oven. Add seasoned shanks. Cook over medium-high heat until meat is brown on both sides; drain.
4. Add 1 cup apple cider; cover tightly and simmer over low heat for 2 hours, turning shanks two or three times.
5. Add carrots, broccoli, potatoes and remaining 1 cup apple cider. Top with sprinkling of brown sugar. Cook, covered, until carrots are crispy tender. (Be careful not to overcook carrots.)

1. To cut venison crosscuts, lay the hind shank on a cutting board, grasp the end of the shank with your free hand and cut 1-inch slices with a meat saw. (It takes a minute or two per shank.) When you're done cutting, be sure to scrape away bone dust and bone chips.

CROSSCUT SHANKS

2. Combine flour, salt and pepper in plastic bag; add crosscut shanks. Shake well; remove shanks.

3. Heat olive oil in Dutch oven. Add seasoned shank; cook over medium heat until meat is brown on both sides; drain.

4. Add 1 cup apple cider; cover tightly and simmer over low heat for 2 hours, turning shanks two or three times.

5. Add carrots, broccoli, potatoes and remaining 1 cup apple cider. Top with sprinkling of brown sugar; cook, covered, until carrots are crispy tender.

Shorter days and a definite chill in the air are true indicators that fall has officially arrived. There's no better time to invite your hunting friends over for a bowl of homemade venison soup.

MEATBALL SOUP

1 1/2 pounds lean ground venison
1/2 cup seasoned bread crumbs
1 egg, beaten
1 teaspoon dried cilantro
Vegetable Spray
2 quarts water
4 beef bouillon cubes, crushed
2 cups frozen green beans, thawed
2 cups frozen whole kernal corn, thawed
1 large onion, diced
3 stalks celery, diced
1/3 cup barley
1 teaspoon salt
1/2 teaspoon black pepper, 1/4 grind (coarse)
1 teaspoon basil
2 (14 1/2-ounce) cans Italian-style stewed tomatoes
2 (6-ounce) cans tomato paste
1 cup Monterey Jack cheese, grated
12 bakery fresh rolls

1. Combine lean ground venison, bread crumbs, egg and cilantro in mixing bowl; mix together well. Shape mixture into 3/4 to 1-inch meatballs.
2. Spray cookie sheet with vegetable spray; add meatballs; bake in preheated 350-degree oven 25 minutes. Remove, set aside.
3. Combine water, bouillon cubes, green beans, corn, onion, celery, barley, salt, pepper, basil, Italian tomatoes and tomato paste in 14-inch Dutch oven; stir well.
4. Add reserved meatballs; cover and simmer 1 hour.
5. Sprinkle each bowl with Monterey Jack cheese and serve with fresh bakery rolls.

Makes 10-12 servings.

While experimenting with different ways to utilize sparerib soup stock, I came up with this wonderful venison chowder.

CHOWDER

6 slices uncooked bacon
3 cups venison stew meat, diced
2 cups fresh mushrooms, halved
4 green onions, diced, tops included
4 1/2 cups venison rib stock, (see page 71)
1 (1.25-ounce) beef soup mix
1/2 teaspoon salt
3/4 teaspoon garlic pepper
2 tablespoons cornstarch
1 1/2 cup zucchini squash, diced
2 stalks celery, diced
1 (16-ounce) can creamed corn
2 cups fresh spinach, chopped
1 (12-ounce) can evaporated milk

1. Fry bacon over medium-high heat in Dutch oven until bacon is crispy brown. Drain all but 2 tablespoons of bacon grease.
2. Stir in diced venison stew meat, mushrooms and onions; cook until onions are crispy tender. Drain pan drippings.
3. Stir in rib stock, beef soup mix, salt and garlic pepper; cook over medium heat, stirring constantly, until slightly thickened. Cover. Reduce heat and simmer 1 hour.
4. Stir in corn starch, zucchini , celery and creamed corn. Simmer over medium heat 15 minutes, stirring frequently.
5. Stir in spinach and evaporated milk; simmer, stirring frequently, until heated through. Be careful not to scorch milk.

Makes 6 servings.

When Mother Nature sends a spell of unseasonably cold weather your way, fight off the chill by building a fire in the cookstove. Then put together a pot of hearty venison soup.

VEGETABLE VENISON SOUP

1 tablespoon olive oil
1 1/2 pounds venison stew meat, diced
2 medium onion, diced
2-3 pounds venison neck bones, with meat
3 quarts water
3 teaspoons salt
2 teaspoons black pepper, 1/4 grind (coarse)
1 medium onion, diced
1 cup barley
1 (8-ounce) can mushroom stems and pieces
3 carrots, sliced
3 medium potatoes, diced
1 (16 ounce) can green beans
1 (28-ounce) can tomato sauce
1 to 2 teaspoons basil (to taste)

1. Heat olive oil in 14-inch Dutch oven; add venison stew meat and onions and cook over medium-high heat until meat is brown on all sides. Drain. Remove meat; reserve.
2. Add venison neck bones, water, salt and pepper; bring to a boil, cover, reduce heat and simmer 2 1/2 to 3 hours or until the meat separates from the bones. Remove bones.
3. Stir in reserved venison and onion, barley, mushroom stems and pieces, carrots, potatoes, green beans, tomato sauce and basil to taste; simmer 40 minutes.

Makes 12 servings.

Having a hunting buddy over for supper? No problem. Plan your meal around a batch of herbed ribs. Sure to please!

HERBED RIB BAKE

4 pounds venison spareribs
Water
1/4 cup catsup
1 (8-ounce) can tomato sauce
1/3 cup brown sugar, packed
1 tablespoon olive oil
2 tablespoons minced onion
1/4 teaspoon rosemary
1/4 teaspoon oregano
1/2 teaspoon basil
1/2 teaspoon coarse black pepper

1. Cut away as much venison tallow from the ribs as possible; use a meat saw to cut ribs into serving-size pieces.
2. Place ribs in pressure cooker; add 3 inches of water and pressure cook at 10 pounds of pressure (follow pressure cooker manufacturer instructions) for 30 minutes.
3. Remove ribs from pressure cooker. drain. Place ribs, meat side up in a shallow baking dish.
4. Combine 1/2 water, catsup, tomato sauce, brown sugar, olive oil, minced onion, rosemary, oregano, basil and pepper in mixing bowl mix well.
5. Pour herb sauce over ribs, cover. Refrigerate 2 hours, turning ribs two or three times.
6. Remove covered ribs from refrigerator and place in preheated 350 degree oven for 1 hour, basting occasionally with herb sauce.

Makes 4 to 6 servings.

Hunters are great at utilizing most of their deer . . . except when it comes to the ribs. Maybe that's because they haven't tasted my excellent Glazed Sparerib recipe.

GLAZED SPARERIBS

4 pounds venison spareribs
1 teaspoon salt
1 (8-ounce) can tomato sauce
1/8 teaspoon cloves, ground
1/2 teaspoon garlic powder or granules
6 drops hot sauce
2 tablespoons Worcestershire sauce
2 tablespoons apple cider vinegar
2 tablespoons brown sugar, packed
1 teaspoon chili powder
1/2 teaspoon dry mustard
1/4 cup raspberry jam

1. Cut away as much venison tallow from the ribs as possible; use a meat saw to cut ribs into serving-size pieces.
2. Place ribs in pressure cooker; add 3 inches of water and pressure-cook at 10 pounds of pressure (follow pressure cooker manufacturer instructions) for 30 minutes.
3. Remove cooked ribs from pressure cooker; set aside, covering to keep warm.
4. Combine salt, tomato sauce, cloves, garlic powder, hot sauce, Worcestershire sauce, vinegar, brown sugar, chili powder, mustard and raspberry jam; simmer 5 minutes, stirring constantly.
5. Baste ribs generously with raspberry mixture; place on grill over hot coals and cook about 6 minutes on each side, basting with remaining raspberry mixture.

Makes 6 servings.

You won't have to apologize for serving venison spareribs when they're pressure-cooked beforehand. Tender and delicious.

SWEET AND SOUR RIBS

4 pounds venison spareribs
1/2 cup flour
1 teaspoon salt
1 tablespoon ginger
4 tablespoons olive oil
1/4 cup apple cider
1/4 cup apple cider vinegar
1/2 cup brown sugar, packed
1/4 cup catsup
1 tablespoon Worcestershire sauce
2 tablespoons soy sauce
2 tablespoons cornstarch
1 (15-ounce) can pineapple chunks, undrained
6 cups hot cooked rice

1. Cut away as much venison tallow from the ribs as possible; use a meat saw to cut ribs into serving-size pieces.
2. Place ribs in pressure cooker, add 3 inches of water and pressure cook at 10 pounds of pressure (follow pressure cooker manufacturer instructions) for 30 minutes.
3. Remove cooked ribs from pressure cooker, cover to keep warm.
4. Combine flour, salt and ginger in medium-size paper sack; add ribs and shake well until ribs are covered with flour mixture.
5. Heat olive oil in Dutch oven; add floured ribs. Cook over medium high heat, turning as needed until ribs are brown on both sides. Remove ribs and set aside. Drain Dutch oven..
6. To make sweet and sour sauce: reduce heat to low, stir in apple cider vinegar, brown sugar, catsup, Worcestershire sauce, soy sauce, cornstarch and pineapple. Simmer, stirring constantly about 5 minutes.
7. Submerge ribs in sauce, turning to cover both sides with sauce. Simmer 30 minutes or until ribs are heated through.
8. Serve with hot cooked rice.

Makes 6 servings.

When Dave and Sharon Taylor host their annual pig roast, they know the spread wouldn't be complete without a steaming pan of venison spareribs smothered in sauerkraut.

SPARERIB-SAUERKRAUT BAKE

4 pounds venison spareribs
Garlic salt
Black pepper, table grind
6 cups tart apples, sliced
1/2 cup onions, diced
1/4 cup brown sugar, packed
1 cup apple cider
1 (32-ounce) bag sauerkraut

1. Cut away as much venison tallow from the ribs as possible; use a meat saw to cut ribs into serving size pieces.
2. Place ribs in pressure cooker; add 3 inches of water and pressure cook at 10 pounds of pressure (follow pressure cooker manufacturer instructions) for 30 minutes.
3. Remove cooked ribs from pressure cooker; sprinkle (to taste) with garlic salt and pepper.
4. Place seasoned ribs in shallow roasting pan; bake in preheated 450-degree oven for 15 minutes to brown ribs. Drain.
5. Top ribs with apple slices, onion slices, brown sugar, apple cider, sauerkraut; cover and bake at 350 degrees for 1 hour.

Makes 6 servings.

Make venison spareribs the highlight of your next evening meal. Top it off with home fries, some sort of creamed vegetables and bakery fresh rolls. You're certain to be a hit!

SMOKY SPARERIBS

4 pounds venison spareribs
Garlic salt
Black pepper, table grind
1/2 cup chili sauce
3/4 cup brown sugar
2 tablespoons apple cider
1 tablespoon lemon juice
1 tablespoon Worcestershire sauce
1 tablespoon chili powder
2 teaspoons hickory smoke flavoring or liquid smoke

1. Cut away as much venison tallow from the ribs as possible.
2. To prepare spareribs: place ribs in pressure cooker. Add 3 inches of water and pressure cook at 10 pounds of pressure (follow pressure cooker manufacturer instructions) for 30 minutes.
3. Remove cooked ribs from pressure cooker; sprinkle (to taste) with garlic salt and pepper. Cover to keep warm.
4. Combine chili sauce, brown sugar, apple cider, lemon juice, Worcestershire sauce, chili powder and hickory smoke flavoring in small sauce pan. Cook over medium heat for 5 minutes, stirring frequently.
5. Place ribs, meat side up, on rack in shallow roasting pan. Baste with sauce. Bake in preheated 350 degree oven for 40 minutes, basting as needed with remaining sauce.
6. Serve while hot with remaining sauce.

Makes 6 servings.

If you're one of the millions of hunters who discard venison spareribs every year because you've heard they're not fit to eat, you owe it to yourself to try one of my sparerib recipes.

HOW TO PREPARE VENISON SPARERIBS

"98 Ways To Enjoy Venison" would be incomplete if I didn't include my favorite sparerib recipes. I've served these scrumptious delights to hunters across the country, almost always to rave reviews. My secret is simple. Conscientious game care from field to table and 30 minutes of pressure cooking.

I can't remember for certain when I first started pressure-cooking venison ribs, but the idea originated with my late grandmother. She used her cooker almost daily, tenderizing meats from beef briskets to old laying hens. Her meals were fork tender and delicious.

Thirty minutes in a pressure cooker transforms otherwise tough and chewy spareribs into a fork-tender delight. Pressure cooking effectively breaks down nearly all the game tallow predominant in most game ribs, producing a lean, tender cut of meat. <u>Skim off the liquid tallow and the resulting broth makes an excellent soup broth.</u> See page 63 for details.

BARBECUED SPARERIBS

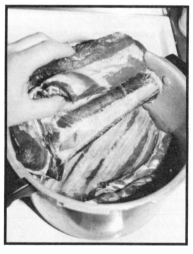

4 pounds venison spareribs
Garlic salt
Black pepper, table grind
1/2 cup butter
1/2 cup catsup
3 tablespoons brown sugar
3 tablespoons lemon juice
2 tablespoons Worcestershire sauce
2 tablespoons steak sauce
6 to 8 drops hot sauce (to taste)
1/4 teaspoon hickory smoke flavor
1/2 cup minced onions

1. Cut away as much tallow from the ribs as possible; place ribs in pressure cooker, add 3 inches of water and pressure-cook according to (pressure cooker) manufacturer instructions for 30 minutes.

BARBECUED SPARERIBS

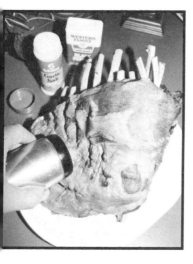

2. Remove cooked ribs from pressure cooker; sprinkle (to taste) with garlic salt and pepper.

3. To make barbecue sauce, Combine butter, catsup, brown sugar, lemon juice, Worcestershire sauce, steak sauce, hot sauce, hickory smoke flavoring and minced onions in sauce pan; stir well. Cook over medium heat 10 minutes, stirring constantly.

4. Place ribs, meat side up, on rack in shallow roasting pan, baste with barbecue sauce and bake uncovered for 30 minutes, basting frequently with sauce.

Makes 6 hearty servings.

If you're an herb lover and want to make your next breakfast extra special, try this recipe. Goes great with eggs, french toast, pancakes, waffles, fried potatoes, etc. (Also fantastic for use in omlets, sausage & biscuits, etc.)

HERBED COUNTRY SAUSAGE

1 pound lean-ground venison
1/2 teaspoon salt
1/4 teaspoon cayenne pepper
1/2 teaspoon dried basil
1/2 teaspoon dried oregano
1/2 teaspoon mustard seed, whole
1/2 teaspoon garlic powder
1/4 cup Parmesan cheese, grated
2 feet of hog casings, rinsed in cold water, soaked overnight

1. Combine lean-ground venison, salt, cayenne pepper, basil, oregano, mustard seed, garlic powder and Parmesan cheese in mixing bowl; mix/knead well.
2. Stuff mixture into hog casings and twist into 4-inch links, or shape mixture into 6-inch diameter sausage patties; refrigerate.
3. Cook, fry, bake or broil as you would any fresh pork sausage.

Makes 4 to 6 servings.

The following venison ham formula is a simple procedure and produces a delicious end product. It's a great way for beginners to delve into home-curing. All you need to get started is ten pounds of venison and ample space in the refrigerator.

BOILED HAM

1 gallon ice water
12 ounces salt
1 1/2 ounces sugar
1 1/2 ounces brown sugar or honey
2 to 3 tablespoons ham/turkey spice (optional)
Non-metallic, deep, brining vessel/crock
10 pounds venison shoulder or round, rolled & tied, chilled
Meat pump or large meat syringe

1. Combine ice water, salt, sugar, brown sugar and ham/turkey spice in non-metallic brining vessel; stir well until salt and sugar are completely dissolved.
2. Fill the meat pump with brine mixture. Insert the meat pump needle to its full length into the chilled venison. Push the pump handle slowly to inject the brine mixture and pump the chilled venison to 10 percent of it's own weight. NOTE: As you force the brine into the chilled venison, slowly retract the pump toward you so the brine mixture is distributed evenly throughout the meat. Repeat this procedure, being sure to penetrate the thickest parts of the meat.
3. To cure: submerge pumped meat in remaining brine mixture (if necessary, place small plate over meat and weight it down with a jar of water). Refrigerate 6 days, turning meat once each day.
4. Remove meat from the brine mixture, rinse and simmer in 165-degree water until the internal temperature of the ham reaches 155 to 160 degrees. The ham is fully cooked at this time. OPTIONAL: For an old-fashioned smokehouse flavor, hang cooked ham in smokehouse. Add smoke chips, smoke/cook at 150-degrees for 2-3 hours and remove
5. Place cooked ham in cold water for 1 to 2 hours to cool; re-frigerate overnight. It's ready to slice and eat the next day.

PEMMICAN

Pemmican is an all but forgotten by-product of jerky which is easily formulated with whole-muscle or restructured jerky. It's exceptionally nutritious and makes a great snack food for home or trail. Old-time pemmican was semi-perishable, particularly those recipes formulated with a high percentage of animal fat. Nor did old timers have freezers to store it in.

Today's pemmican, formulated without animal fat, will keep for 6 months to a year without breaking down. It has a delicious, pleasing flavor that easily satisfies one's immediate hunger. Now, with peanut butter successfully replacing animal fat as a base, today's pemmican will keep for longer periods of time. It's also delicious. **Try the following recipe and see how you like it.** If you want to make changes, try adding one (or a combination) of your favorite spices. You can also try different dried fruits. Keep experimenting until you find a combination that suits your taste.

PEMMICAN

4	ounces venison jerky
4	ounces raisins
3	ounces currants, dried
6	tablespoons peanut butter smooth or crunchy
2	tablespoons honey, warm
1/4	teaspoon cayenne pepper, more pepper is optional

1. To make pemmican: grind jerky, raisins and currants twice through the 3/16-inch plate of a meat grinder.
2. Combine jerky/raisin mixture with peanut butter, honey and cayenne pepper; mix well with spoon until thick and pasty.
3. Roll mixture into 1-inch balls, cool, and store in freezer until needed. Well last up to two weeks on countertop.

   Yields 1 pound of pemmican.

Here's a couple of ideas for your fresh-made pastrami. Both recipes use rye bread or crackers as accents.

PASTRAMI SPREAD

1 (8-ounce) package Neufchatel cheese, softened
1/4 cup butter
1 teaspoon paprika
8 ounces pastrami, shredded
2 green onions, including tops, diced
1/4 teaspoon cayenne pepper
1 teaspoon caraway seeds, whole
Vegetable spray

1. Beat Neufchatel cheese, butter and paprika with electric mixer at medium speed until smooth and fluffy.
2. Stir in shredded pastrami, onions, cayenne pepper and caraway seeds; mix well.
3. Spray vegetable spray on inside surface of 16-ounce jello mold; pack cheese/pastrami spread firmly into mold.
4. Cover; refrigerate overnight. The next day, invert the spread onto a serving dish and serve with rye bread squares or rye crackers.

REUBEN SANDWICHES

8 slices rye bread
Thousand Island dressing
1 cup sauerkraut, drained well
4 (1-ounce) slices Swiss cheese
8 ounces pastrami, shredded

1. Lay out 8 slices rye bread; spread each slice generously with thousand island dressing.
2. Layer sauerkraut, Swiss cheese and pastrami on bottom half of bread. Cover with remaining bread slices, Thousand Island side down; bake at 350 degrees for 15 minutes, or until cheese melts.

Makes 4 servings.

The next time your hunting partner's freezer goes on the blink and you inherit a bunch of leftover meat, you might want to thaw some of the larger cuts and try your luck at making pastrami.

PASTRAMI

2 quarts cold water
6 teaspoons curing salt (quick cure, prague powder, etc.)
1 cup table salt
1/2 cup dextrose
2 tablespoons garlic powder
Meat Pump
10 pounds venison round (top or bottom)
4 tablespoons black pepper, coarse ground
4 tablespoons coriander, ground
4 tablespoons paprika

1. Combine 2 quarts cold water, curing salt, table salt, dextrose and garlic powder in ample-size non-metallic brining vessel; stir well.
2. Fill meat pump or syringe with brine mixture and pump meat to 12 to 15 percent of its green weight. To submerge meat in brine: Place small plate over meat and weight down with a jar of water.
3. To cure pumped meat, refrigerate 6 days, turning meat once each day.
4. Remove cured meat from brine; drip dry.
5. Mix together coarse black pepper, coriander and paprika. Rub all sides of cured meat with seasoning mixture.
6. Insert meat thermometer into center of rubbed meat. Place meat on cookie sheet in preheated 200 degree oven and bake for one hour with oven door cracked slightly open.
7. Close oven door and bake at 200 degrees until internal temperature of pastrami reaches 165 degrees; remove from oven. Cool slightly.
8. Slice finished pastrami into thin pieces and serve on rye bread with mustard and horseradish.

Makes about 6 pounds of venison pastrami. You can expect a 40 to 50 percent shrinkage from the green weight of the meat.

Because one-dish casseroles are easy to make and require little attention during cooking, they're the perfect choice for after work meals.

CORNED MEAT CASSEROLE

1 pound corned venison (see page 79)
Vegetable spray
1 (10 3/4-ounce) can cream of mushroom soup, undiluted
1 (10 1/2-ounce) can French onion soup, undiluted
2 cups milk
1 (8-ounce) package noodles, cooked
8 ounces Velveeta cheese
1/4 cup Italian bread crumbs

1. Grind corned venison one time through 3/8" coarse plate of meat chopper (meat grinder).
2. Spray deep baking dish with vegetable spray.
3. Mix together ground corned venison, cream of mushroom soup, French onion soup, milk and cooked noodles.
4. Pour mixture in prepared baking dish; top with Velveeta cheese and Italian bread crumbs. Bake, uncovered, in preheated 350-degree oven for 45 minutes, or until casserole is hot and bubbly.

Makes 4 servings.

Now that you've made your first crock of corned meat, you can try one of the following recipes. This one is venison at its best.

CORNED MEAT AND CABBAGE

6 cups water
3 pounds corned venison, (see page 79)
8 new potatoes, medium size, unpeeled, halved
4 medium carrots, quartered
2 medium yellow onions, quartered
1 medium head cabaage, quartered

1. Pour water into Dutch oven; add corned venison. Cover, simmer 45 minutes, or until corned venison is heated through.
2. Add new potatoes, carrots and yellow onions; cook, covered, over medium heat 10 minutes.
3. Add cabbage; cook, covered, 15 to 20 minutes, or until cabbage is crispy tender.

Makes 8 servings.

CORNED MEAT SANDWICHES

1/2 pound corned venison (see page 79)
1/4 cup celery, diced
1/4 cup onions, diced
1 teaspoon prepared mustard
1/2 teaspoon prepared horseradish
1/4 cup mayonnaise
4 hard rolls, split, toasted

1. Shred (slice very thin) corned venison.
2. Combine shredded corned venison, celery, onions, mustard, horse radish and mayonnaise in small mixing bowl; mix well.
3. Spread mixture on bottom half of each toasted hard roll; cover with top of hard roll.

Makes 4 servings.

Hunters! If you're sucessful this season, you might want to put aside at least ten pounds of venison shoulder to cure a crock of corned meat.

CORNED MEAT

2 quarts cold water
6 teaspoons curing salt (quick cure, prague powder, etc.)
1 cup table salt
1/3 cup dextrose
2 tablespoons garlic powder
1 tablespoon black pepper, table grind
10 pounds venison shoulder, whole or chunks
Meat Pump
Non-metallic brining vessel
2 tablespoons pickling spice

1. Combine 2 quarts water, curing salt, table salt, dextrose, garlic powder and black pepper in ample-size, non-metallic brining vessel/crock; stir well.
2. Fill meat pump or syringe with brine mixture and pump meat to 12 to 15 percent of its green weight with brine. Submerge meat in brine (if necessary, place small plate over meat and weight down with a jar of water).
3. To cure pumped meat: refrigerate 6 days, turning meat once each day.
4. Remove cured meat from brine, rinse gently with cold water and place in heavy kettle. Add enough fresh water to cover. Add pickling spice, cover and simmer 3 to 4 hours, turning occasion ally until corned meat is tender.
5. Ready to eat.

Makes about 6 pounds of corned venison. Note: you can expect a 40-50 percent shrinkage from the green weight of the meat.

Looking for a good recipe to sample your freshly-made dried venison? Your timing couldn't be better to try this old-fashioned delight. Creamed Venison is easy to make and mighty tasty.

CREAMED VENISON

1 pound smoked/dried venison (see pages 81-82)
2 tablespoons olive oil
1 bouillin cube, crushed
5 tablespoons flour
3 cups milk
1/4 teaspoon white pepper
1 tablespoon dried parsley
6 slices thick-crusted bread, toasted
Parmesean cheese

1. Shred (thin slice) dried venison into small pieces.
2. Heat olive oil in large skillet, add bouillon cube and shredded dried venison; cook over medium-high heat until edges of dried venison begin to curl and brown. Drain excess oil.
3. Sprinkle flour over dried venison and allow to brown slightly.
4. Stir in milk, white pepper, dried parsley and simmer over low heat, stirring constantly until smooth and thickened; remove from heat.
5. Serve over toasted bread; top each serving with sprinkle of Parmesan cheese.

Makes 4 servings.

PROPORTIONED VENISON MEAT YIELD FROM 158 POUND WHITETAIL DEER
HANGING (CARCASS) WEIGHT 115 POUNDS

	Hanging Weight 115 lbs.	Steaks & Roasts	Burger & Sausage Trim	Waste (Fat & Bones)
Hind Shanks	6 lbs.	none	3 lbs.	2 lbs.
Rounds	16 lbs.	3 lbs. Rump Roast 4 lbs. Round Steak 2 lbs. Finger Steak	3 lbs.	4 lbs.
Sirloin Tips	7 lbs.	1 1/2 lbs. Sandwich Steak 3 lbs. Sirloin Tip Steak 1/2 lb. Bite-Size Steak	1/2 lb.	1 1/2 lb.
Rumps	4 lbs.	3 lbs. Rump Roast	1/2 lb.	1/2 lb.
Sirloins	6 lbs.	3 lbs. Sirloin Steaks 1 lb. Bite-Size Steaks	1/4 lb.	1 3/4 lb.
Flanks	2 lbs.	none	1 lb.	1 lb.
Loin Half Backstraps	5 lbs.	4 lbs. Butterfly Steaks	3/4 lb.	1/4 lb.
Tenderloins	3 lbs.	1 1/2 lbs. Whole Tenderloin	none	1 1/2 lbs.
Plates Spareribs	11 lbs.	6 lbs. Spareribs	3 lbs.	2 lbs.
Rib Half Backstraps	16 lbs.	6 lbs. Stand/Rib Roast 6 lbs. rib chops	1 lb.	3 lb.
Briskets	2 lbs.	none	1 lb.	1 lb.
Chucks (Shoulders)	19 lbs.	6 lbs. Shoulder Roast 2 lbs. Stew Meat	6 lbs.	5 lbs.
Foreshanks	3 lbs.	none	2 lbs.	1 lb
Neck	16 lbs.	4 lbs. Neck roast 2 lbs. Stew Meat	5 1/2 lbs.	4 1/2 lbs.
Total Yield	115 lbs.	68 1/2 lbs.	27 1/2 lbs.	29 lbs.

The 86-lb. yield from the above 158 pound deer is about normal for what you would expect from a healthy whitetail deer. Generally, the yield is about half of the live-weight of deer, elk, moose, caribou, antelope, etc. However, poor shot placement and less than conscientious field care, starting the moment an animal is down, reduces the yield further, as much as an additional 50 percent in some cases.

There's a number of other factors that cut into the yield. Where was the deer hung? How long did it hang before it was processed.? What was the temperature? Did the temperature flucuate, etc.

I can't stress enough when the moment comes to pull the trigger, wait for the right shot. Take your time and don't make a mistake that you'll regret. There's always another day afield and another deer to chase. Searching hopelessly for a mortally wounded animal doesn't build pleasant memories. If you're gifted with a conscience , you'll live with your careless mistake the rest of your life.

I'm strictly a meat hunter. and I honestly prefer venison over beef. I savor every moment afield and when I see a buck sneaking through the woods, I'm not thinking about a trophy rack to hang over the fire place mantel. Instead, I'm envisioning hickory-grilled rounds, honey-baked chops and inch-thick burgers. I choose my animal and my shot carefully so my highly-prized gamemeat is the best it can be.

Making homemade dried meat is a fading tradition in many parts of the country, mostly because the age-old process isn't being passed on.

DRIED VENISON

2 quarts water
6 teaspoons curing salt (quick cure, prague powder, etc.)
1 cup table salt
1/2 cup brown sugar
2 tablespoons white pepper
2 tablespoons garlic powder or granules
10 pounds venison round, top or bottom
Meat pump
Non-metallic brining vessel

1. Combine 2 quarts water, curing salt, table salt, brown sugar, white pepper, and garlic powder in large, non-metallic sauce pot; bring to a boil, stirring constantly.
2. Remove brine mixture from heat; cool.
3. Pour cooled brine mixture into stoneware crock, glass container or smaller food-grade plastic bucket.
4. Fill meat pump or syringe with brine mixture and pump meat to 12 to15 percent of its green weight with brine; submerge meat in brine (if necessary, place small plate over meat and weight down with a jar of water). Refrigerate 6 days, turning meat once a day.
5. Place meat on bacon hook, or place in stockinette. Hang in pre-heated smoker (damper open) and process at 130-140 degrees for 1 hour or until the surface of the meat is dry to the touch. Close damper, add smoke chips and increase heat to 150-160 degrees for 2-3 hours. Then increase heat to 200 degrees and hold until the internal temperature of the meat reaches 175 degrees. Hang meat at room temperature to cool.
6. At this time, product is fully cooked and ready to eat. Dried venison can be refrigerated up to two weeks or double-wrapped and frozen up to one year.
   To process in oven, lay cured venison on oven rack, crack open oven door slightly. Turn heat to lowest setting for 1 hour. Close door, increase heat to 200 degrees and hold until the internal temperature of the meat reaches 175 degrees. Hang meat at room temperature to cool.

When I think of old-fashioned meat pies like grandma used to make, the first thing that comes to mind is her renowned potato pie crusts. The following is a close rendition of her best.

BURGER POT PIE

2 pounds hash browns
1 egg, beaten
1 tablespoon granulated onion
1/2 teaspoon salt
1 tablespoon olive oil
1 pound lean-ground venison
1 (16-ounce) can whole kernel corn, undrained
1 (16-ounce) can green beans, undrained
1 (10-ounce) can tomato soup, undiluted
1/3 teaspoon oregano
1/3 teaspoon black pepper, table grind
1 tablespoon sugar
1 cup Monterey Jack cheese, grated

1. Combine hash browns, egg, granulated onion and salt in mixing bowl; toss lightly.
2. Press hash-brown mixture into greased 9-inch deep pie plate to form crust; bake crust in preheated 400-degree oven for 15-20 minutes, remove and set aside.
3. Heat olive oil in skillet; add lean-ground venison. Cook over medium-high heat until venison is browned, stirring frequently to crumble; drain and set aside.
4. Combine corn, green beans, tomato soup, oregano, pepper and sugar in mixing bowl; stir well.
5. Pour filling mixture into hash-brown pastry; bake in preheated 400-degree oven for 20 minutes. Remove, top with sprinkling of Monterey Jack cheese and bake an additional 5 minutes or until cheese is melted and light golden brown.
6. Cool slightly and cut into 6 pieces.

Makes 6 servings.

Looking for a new way to use up last year's ground venison? A skillet of Burger Hash might be the answer. And you can make it as spicy as you'd like by simply alternating the style of Picante sauce you use.

BURGER HASH

1 tablespoon olive oil
1 pound lean-ground venison
1 medium onion, diced
1 green bell pepper, diced
1 beef bouillon cube, crushed
2 tablespoons hot water
1/2 teaspoon salt
1/2 teaspoon black pepper, coarse ground
4 medium potatoes, unpeeled, diced
4 eggs
Picante sauce
Catsup

1. Heat olive oil in deep skillet, add lean-ground venison, onion and bell pepper; cook over medium-high heat until venison is browned, stirring frequently to crumble. Drain.
2. Stir in bouillon cube, hot water, salt, black pepper and diced potatoes. Cover. Simmer 20 minutes, stirring frequently, or until potatoes are tender.
3. Top with eggs; cover. Simmer additional 1-2 minutes or until eggs reach the desired degree of doneness.
4. Serve with medium-heat Picante sauce or catsup.

Makes 4 servings.

This is a great dish to make ahead and take to camp. It's nutritious and delicious, as well as an easy meal to serve after a long day of hunting or fishing.

BURGER AND BEANS

2 tablespoons olive oil
2 pounds lean-ground venison
2 large yellow onions, chopped
2 (15-ounce) cans butter beans
1 (15.5-ounce) can red kidney beans
1 (15-ounce) can pork and beans in tomato sauce
3/4 cup brown sugar, packed
1 tablespoon molasses
1 tablespoon mustard powder
2 teaspoons salt
1 teaspoon black pepper, coarse ground
2 teaspoons red wine vinegar
1/2 cup catsup

1. Heat olive oil in Dutch oven; add lean-ground venison. Cook over medium-high heat until venison is browned, stirring frequently to crumble; drain.
2. Stir in onions, butter beans, red kidney beans, pork and beans, brown sugar, molasses, mustard powder, salt, black pepper, red wine vinegar and catsup. Cover and bake in preheated 350-degree oven, or cook over hot coals for 45 minutes.

Makes 12 to 14 servings.

Unless you're anti-social, it's a safe bet you'll be invited to a potluck dinner within the next year. That will be a great time to take along a batch of my venison cocktail meatballs.

COCKTAIL MEATBALLS

2 tablespoons olive oil
1 large onion, diced
1 medium bell pepper, seeded, diced
1 teaspoon garlic powder
2 pounds lean-ground venison
4 slices white bread, crumbled
2 eggs, beaten
1 1/2 teaspoon salt
1/2 teaspoon white pepper
1/4 cup Italian dressing, oil based
1 cup currant jelly
1 1/2 cup chili sauce
2 tablespoons cornstarch
1 (8-ounce) can crushed pineapple, undrained

1. Heat olive oil in large skillet; add onion, bell pepper and garlic powder. Cook over medium-high heat until onion is crispy tender; drain.
2. Combine lean-ground venison, cooked onion mixture, bread, eggs, salt, white pepper and Italian dressing in large mixing bowl; mix well and shape into small (3/4-1-inch) meatballs.
3. Place meatballs in shallow baking dish. Bake meatballs in pre heated 350-degree oven for 25 minutes or until cooked through; cover. Set aside.
4. Combine currant jelly, chili sauce, cornstarch and crushed pine-apple; stir well. Cook over medium heat until thickened, stirring constantly.
5. Pour sauce over meatballs; bake in preheated 300-degree oven for 20 minutes.
6. Serve hot with wooden picks.

Makes 4 to 5 dozen cocktail appetizers.

If your schedule is hectic and you want something you can put together fast, the following recipe could be what you're looking for. It's simple and cheesy delicious.

BURGER & CHEESE CASSEROLE

2 tablespoons olive oil
1 pound lean-ground venison
1 medium onion, chopped
1 green bell pepper, seeded, chopped
1 (4-ounce) can mushroom stems and pieces, drained
1 (15-ounce) can butter beans
1 (28-ounce) can tomatoes, undrained, chopped
1 (6-ounce) can tomato paste
6 cups (8 ounces) noodles, cooked
1/2 teaspoon basil
1/2 teaspoon salt
1/4 teaspoon cayenne pepper
2 cups cottage cheese
8 ounces Velveeta cheese
Paprika

. Heat olive oil in Dutch oven; add lean-ground venison, onion, bell pepper and mushroom stems and pieces. Cook over medium-high heat, stirring frequently until venison is browned and onions are crispy tender; drain.
. Stir in butter beans, tomatoes, tomato paste, noodles, salt, pepper and cottage cheese. Top with Velveeta cheese, sprinkle with paprika, and bake in preheated 400-degree oven for 20-25 minutes or until hot and bubbly.

Makes 6 servings.

When it's my wife's turn to cook, she nearly always chooses a one-dish casserole. She says they're easy to put together and she doesn't dirty a lot of dishes in the process.

SAUSAGE CASSEROLE

1 pound ground venison
1 small onion, diced
1/2 green bell pepper, seeded, diced
1 teaspoon coriander, cut
1 teaspoon thyme
1/2 teaspoon black pepper, coarse-ground
1 teaspoon sugar
1/2 teaspoon salt
1/2 teaspoon garlic granules or powder
1 (10 3/4-ounce) can cream of mushroom soup, undiluted
1 (10 3/4-ounce) can cream of celery soup, undiluted
3 cups water
1 cup uncooked long-grain rice
Paprika

1. Combine ground venison, onion, bell pepper, coriander, thyme, pepper, sugar, salt, and garlic in mixing bowl; mix/knead well.
2. Shape sausage mixture into 2-inch patties; cook patties in Dutch oven, stirring frequently to brown patties on both sides. Drain; set sausage patties aside.
3. Combine cream of mushroom soup, cream of celery soup, water and long-grain rice in Dutch oven. Bring to a boil, cover, reduce heat and simmer 5 minutes.
4. Gently stir in sausage patties, sprinkle with paprika, cover and bake in preheated 350-degree oven for 25 minutes.

Makes 6 servings.

Sausage gravy and biscuits may be one of the West's best kept secrets. The following rendition features freshly made country sausage and buttermilk biscuits.

SAUSAGE AND BISCUITS

1 pound ground venison
1/2 teaspoon salt
1 teaspoon thyme
1/4 teaspoon cayenne pepper
2 1/2 cups flour
2 teaspoons baking powder
1/2 teaspoon baking soda
1/2 teaspoon salt
2 teaspoons dried parsley flakes
2 teaspoons Parmesan cheese, grated

1/3 cup shortening	1/3 cup flour
1 1/4 cup buttermilk	3 1/4 cups milk

1. Combine ground venison, salt, thyme and cayenne pepper in mixing bowl; mix well. Refrigerate.
2. Combine 2 1/2 cups flour, baking powder, baking soda, salt, parsley and Parmesan cheese in large mixing bowl; cut in shortening.
3. Add buttermilk, stirring until dry ingredients are moistened. Turn out onto a lightly floured surface; knead gently about 1 minute.
4. Roll dough to 3/4-inch thickness; cut with biscuit cutter.
5. Place biscuits on lightly greased cookie sheet; bake in preheated 425-degree oven for 8 minutes. Brush biscuit tops with butter. Bake an additional 5 minutes or until golden brown; set aside.
6. Cook sausage mixture in large skillet until browned, stirring frequently to crumble sausage; drain.
7. Stir in 1/3 cup flour and 3 1/4 cups milk; cook over medium-low heat, stirring constantly until thickened.
8. Split hot biscuits open; top with sausage gravy.

Makes 6 man-size servings.

Sloppy Joes are a natural choice for cool-weather days. This new version is easy to make and great tasting too.

SLOPPY JOES

2 tablespoons olive oil
1 pound lean-ground venison
1 small onion
1 medium green bell pepper, seeded and chopped
1 (14 1/2-ounce) can stewed tomatoes
1 (6-ounce) can tomato paste
1 tablespoon red wine vinegar
1 tablespoon Worcestershire sauce
1 tablespoon prepared mustard
1/2 teaspoon garlic powder
1/4 teaspoon salt
1/4 teaspoon white pepper
1 loaf French bread, sliced lengthwise, lightly toasted
1 cup mozzarella cheese, grated, divided into fourths
Parmesan cheese

1. Heat olive oil in Dutch oven; add lean-ground venison, onion and bell pepper. Cook over medium-high heat until venison is browned, stirring frequently to crumble venison; drain.
2. Stir in stewed tomatoes, tomato paste, red wine vinegar, Worcestershire sauce, mustard, garlic powder, salt and white pepper; simmer, uncovered for 25 minutes, stirring frequently.
3. Remove sloppy joe (meat) mixture from heat; cover and set aside.
4. Cut toasted French bread into 4 equal portions. Top each bottom portion with 1/4 of mozzarella cheese and 1/8 of meat mixture. Add top of bread, cover with 1/8 of meat mixture and sprinkle with Parmesan cheese. Repeat mixture with remaining bread portions.

Makes 4 serving.

I tasted a true Stromboli in Harrisburg, Pennsylvania, while exhibiting at the Eastern Sportsman Show, and it was absolutely delicious. My venison-based rendition isn't bad, either.

STROMBOLI

2 tablespoons olive oil
1 pound lean-ground venison
1 medium onion, chopped
1 bell pepper, seeded, chopped
1 (4-ounce) can mushroom stems and pieces, drained
2 (16-ounce) loaves frozen bread dough, thawed
Italian salad dressing, oil based
12 slices American cheese
12 slices mozzarella cheese
1/2 pound pepperoni, sliced thinly
Italian seasoning
Spaghetti sauce

1. Heat olive oil in skillet, add lean-ground venison, onion, bell pepper and mushrooms. Cook over medium-high heat until venison is browned, stirring frequently to crumble venison. Drain; set aside.
2. Using a lightly floured surface, roll each loaf of bread dough into roughly 16" x 8" pastry shells. Cut each shell into halves.
3. Spread surface of first 8" x 8" shell half with a light brushing of Italian dressing, top one half of oiled surface with venison/onion mixture, 3 slices American cheese, 3 slices mozzarella cheese, 1/4 of pepperoni slices and a sprinkle of Italian seasoning; repeat procedure with remaining shells.
4. Fold empty side of dough shell over meat/cheese; press edges to seal dough on all sides. Repeat procedure with remaining shells.
5. Brush outside surface of shells with a light brushing of Italian dressing; bake shells in preheated 350-degree oven for 30 to 35 minutes or until shells are golden brown.
6. Serve with bowl of spaghetti sauce.

Makes 4 servings.

If you're tired of the same old soup recipe, try this unusual recipe, featuring lean-ground venison and mushrooms.

BURGER SOUP

1 tablespoon olive oil
1 pound lean-ground venison
1 pound fresh mushrooms, halved
3 green onions, including tops, chopped
2 cloves garlic, minced
2 tablespoons cornstarch
1 (10 1/2-ounce) can beef broth
1 cup milk
1 (10-ounce) package frozen corn, thawed
1 (10-ounce) package frozen peas, thawed
1/2 teaspoon salt
1/2 teaspoon black pepper, table grind
1/4 teaspoon basil
1/4 teaspoon thyme
6 slices Swiss cheese

1. Heat olive oil in Dutch oven; add lean-ground venison, mushrooms, green onions and garlic. Cook over medium heat until venison is browned, stirring frequently to crumble venison; drain. Reduce heat.
2. Stir in cornstarch, beef broth, milk, corn, peas, salt, pepper, basil and thyme; cover and simmer over low heat for 20 minutes.
3. Serve hot soup in bowl; top each bowl with a slice of Swiss cheese.

Makes 6 servings.

When deciding what to cook for your next meal, you might want to take a look at this recipe.

SWEET & SOUR MEATBALLS

1 pound lean-ground venison
3 slices white bread, crumbled
1 egg, beaten
1/3 teaspoon salt
1/3 teaspoon marjoram
2 tablespoons olive oil
4 green onions, including tops, diced
1 medium green bell pepper, diced
1 medium red pepper, diced
1 (15 1/2-ounce) can pineapple chunks, undrained
1/3 cup apple cider vinegar
1/3 cup catsup
1/3 cup sugar
2 tablespoons soy sauce
2 tablespoons cornstarch
4 cups hot cooked rice

1. Combine lean-ground venison, bread, egg, salt and marjoram in a large mixing bowl; mix/knead thoroughly.
2. Shape mixture into 1-inch diameter meat balls.
3. Place meatballs on cookie sheet in preheated 375-degree oven; Bake 30 minutes or until meatballs are cooked through; set aside.
4. Heat olive oil in large skillet; add onions and bell peppers. Cook over medium heat until onions are crispy tender. stirring frequently; drain.
5. Stir in pineapple chunks/juice, vinegar, catsup, sugar, soy sauce, cornstarch and meatballs. Bring mixture to a boil, reduce heat and simmer 7 minutes or until meat balls are heated through.
6. Serve over hot cooked rice.

Makes 4 servings.

When the weather cools and thoughts turn to whitetail bucks and bull elk, it's time to get out the Dutch oven and put together a hearty gumbo.

GUMBO

2 tablespoons olive oil
2 pounds lean-ground venison
1 large onion, chopped
2 stalks celery, chopped
2 cloves garlic, minced
1 (14 1/2-ounce) can stewed tomatoes
1 (15-ounce) can tomato sauce
2 (6-ounce) cans tomato paste
1 (8-ounce) can mushroom stems and pieces, drained
1 cup frozen corn
1 teaspoon basil
1 teaspoon Italian seasoning
1 teaspoon oregano
1 teaspoon cumin
1 teaspoon chili powder
1 teaspoon salt
1/2 teaspoon cayenne pepper
2 medium zucchini squash, chopped
8 cups hot cooked rice

1. Heat olive oil in Dutch oven; add lean-ground venison, onion, celery and garlic. Cook over medium heat until venison is browned, stirring frequently to crumble venison; drain.
2. Stir in stewed tomatoes, tomato sauce, tomato paste, mushroom stems and pieces, corn, basil, Italian seasoning, oregano, cumin, chili powder, salt and cayenne pepper.
3. Simmer, uncovered, 50 minutes; stir in zucchini squash. Simmer an additional 10 minutes, stirring occasionally.
4. Serve over hot cooked rice.

Makes 8 servings.

Cooking the evening meal can be a bummer, especially when you've had a stressful day at work. This tasty one-dish meal takes less than 45 minutes from start to finish.

COUNTRY CASSEROLE

3 tablespoons olive oil
2 pounds lean-ground venison
1 medium onion, chopped
2 cloves garlic, minced
1 (15-ounce) can tomato sauce
1 (6-ounce) can tomato paste
1 teaspoon black pepper, coarse ground
1 teaspoon salt
1 teaspoon oregano
2 teaspoons Italian seasoning
1 (16 oounce) can whole kernel corn
1 medium cabbage, shredded
1 medium zucchini squash, cut into 3/4-inch chunks
1 large yellow summer squash, cut into 3-inch chunks
8 ounces Velveeta cheese

1. Heat olive oil in Dutch oven; add lean-ground venison, onion and minced garlic. Cook over medium heat until venison is browned, stirring frequently to crumble venison; drain.
2. Stir tomato sauce, tomato paste, pepper, salt, oregano and Italian seasoning into venison mixture; mix well. Simmer 10 minutes, stirring frequently.
3. Stir in whole kernel corn, cabbage, zucchini and summer squash; cover. Simmer/cook over medium heat about 30 minutes or until cabbage is crispy tender.
4. Top with Velveeta cheese, cover and simmer an additional 5 minutes or until cheese is bubbly.

Makes 8 servings.

Ground venison is an excellent meat, richly flavored, high in protein and low in fat. It goes well with any kind of pasta recipe.

MEATBALL FETTUCCINE

1 pound lean-ground venison
1 egg, beaten
1 cup croutons
1 tablespoon granulated onion
1/2 teaspoon seasoning salt
3 to 4 drops hot sauce
2 (4 ounce) cans mushroom stems and pieces, drained
1 (1.25-ounce) envelope beef flavored soup mix, divided
2 tablespoons flour
1 1/4 cup water
1 cup sour cream
4 cups hot-cooked fettuccine

1. Combine lean-ground venison, egg, croutons, granulated onion, seasoning salt, hot sauce, 1 can mushroom stems and pieces and 1/2 envelope of soup mix; mix well. Shape into small meatballs.
2. Place meatballs on greased cookie sheet; bake, uncovered, in preheated 350-degree oven 20 to 25 minutes, or until meatballs reach the desired degree of doneness. Set aside.
3. Combine flour, remaining soup mix and water in large skillet, stirring constantly; cook over medium heat until smooth and thickened.
4. Stir in sour cream and remaining can mushroom stems and pieces. Add meatballs; cook over medium-low heat 3-5 minutes or until heated through, stirring constantly.
5. Serve over hot fettuccine.

Makes 4 servings.

If you have an abundance of ground venison and you're running out of creativity, try a batch of venison burritos.

BURRITOS

1 tablespoon olive oil
1 pound lean-ground venison
1 small onion, diced
1 small clove garlic, minced, or 1/2 teaspoon garlic powder
1 (8-ounce) can mushroom stems and pieces, drained
1/3 teaspoon oregano
1/3 teaspoon ground cumin
1 (8-ounce) package cream cheese, softened
4 (9-inch) flour tortillas
1 (14 1/2 ounce) can stewed tomatoes
8 medium Peperoncini, stemed and seeded
1 teaspoon cornstarch
1 teaspoon sugar
1 teaspoon bazil
5 cups lettuce, shredded
1 cup green onions or fresh chives, chopped
1 cup sour cream, separated into fourths

1. Heat olive oil in large skillet; add, venison, onion, minced garlic, mushroom stems and pieces. Cook over medim-high heat until venison is browned, stirring frequently to crumble; drain.
2. Reduce heat, add bazil, oregano, cumin and cream cheese; stir well until blended, remove from heat.
3. Fill each tortilla equally with beef/cheese mixture; roll up and place seam side down in ample-size, greased baking dish.
4. Cover and bake in preheated 350-degree oven for 20 minutes.
5. To make tomato sauce: combine stewed tomatoes, Peperoncini, cornstarch, sugar and basil in blender; blend until smooth.
Pour mixture into saucepan, bring to a boil and simmer 3 minutes.
6. Top each burrito with cooked tomato sauce,1/2 cup shredded lettuce, 2 to 3 tablespoons chopped green onions and 2 to 3 table-spoons sour cream.

Makes 4 servings.

If you think all burgers are alike, think again. The following sour cream version is definitely different and super tasty.

SOUR CREAM BURGERS

1 tablespoon butter
1 small onion, diced
1/4 cup sour cream
1 egg, beaten
1/4 teaspoon mustard seed
1/8 teaspoon ground mustard
1/8 teaspoon ground majoram
2 slices soft white bread, crumbled
4 to 5 drops Tobasco sauce, more is optional
1 pound lean-ground venison
4 hamburger rolls, toasted
4 slices Swiss cheese

1. Heat butter in small sauce pan; add onion. Cook over medium-high heat until onion is crispy tender, drain, and place cooked onion in mixing bowl.
2. Stir in sour cream, egg, mustard seed, ground mustard, majoram, bread and Tobasco sauce. Add lean-ground venison; mix well.
3. Shape meat mixture into 4 separate 3/4-inch thick burgers; bake or broil 6 to 7 minutes on each side or until the burgers reach the desired degree of doneness.
4. Place hot-grilled burgers on bottoms of toasted hamburger rolls.
5. Top each burger with 1 slice of Swiss cheese and top of roll.

Makes 4 servings.

With so many excellent lasagna recipes to choose from, you may have trouble deciding on a favorite one. The following has great flavor and uses lean-ground venison as the base.

LASAGNA

1 tablespoon olive oil
1 pound lean-ground venison
2 cloves garlic, minced
1 large onion, diced
1 (14 1/2-ounce) can stewed tomatoes, undrained
2 (6-ounce) cans tomato paste
1 1/2 cup water
2 teaspoons oregano
1 teaspoon salt
1/4 teaspoon white pepper
2 cups ricotta cheese
1 large egg, beaten
1 (8-ounce) carton sour cream
1 1/2 cups mozzarella cheese, grated, divided in thirds
1/2 cup Parmesan cheese, divided in thirds
12 lasagna noodles, cooked

1. Heat olive oil in Dutch oven. add venison, garlic and onion. Cook over medium heat until venison is browned, stirring frequently to crumble venison; drain.
2. Stir in stewed tomatoes, tomato paste, water, oregano, salt and white pepper; simmer, uncovered, 1 hour, stirring frequently.
3. Meanwhile, combine ricotta cheese, egg and sour cream in small mixing bowl; mix well and set aside.
4. Arrange 4 lasagna noodles in bottom of large, deep baking dish; top with 1/3 of cooked meat mixture, ricotta cheese mixture, 1/2 cup mozzarella cheese and 1/3 of Parmesan cheese. Repeat procedure with remaining ingredients.
5. Bake at 350 degrees for 45 minutes or until bubbly.
6. Let stand 10 to 15 minutes; serve with toasted garlic bread.

Makes 8 servings.

Most people love pizza, and whom among the masses can resist a good burger. This recipe combines the best of both.

PIZZA PIE

1 tablespoon olive oil
1 1/2 pounds lean-ground venison
1 large onion, chopped
1 medium bell pepper, chopped
2 cloves garlic, minced
1 (14 1/2-ounce) can stewed tomatoes, undrained
1 (6-ounce) can tomato paste
1 (8-ounce) can mushroom stems and pieces, drained
1/2 teaspoon chili powder
1/2 teaspoon cayenne pepper
1 tablespoon oregano

2 cups flour	1 tablespoon baking powder
1/2 teaspoon salt	1/4 cup shortening
3/4 cup milk	2 tablespoons dried parsley

1. Heat olive oil in Dutch oven; add lean-ground venison, onion, bell pepper and garlic, stirring to crumble venison.
2. Cook over medium heat, stirring, until onion is tender; drain.
3. Add stewed tomatoes, tomato paste, mushroom stems and pieces, chili powder, cayenne pepper and oregano to venison mixture. Simmer 25 minutes, stirring frequently; set aside.
4. To make pastry: combine flour, baking powder and salt in mixing bowl; stir. Cut in shortening; add milk and parsley.
5. Stir pastry mixture lightly until mixed. Place two thirds of pastry into large baking dish; form into pastry shell.
6. Pour venison/tomato mixture into pastry shell; sprinkle top evenly with mozzarella cheese. Top with remaining pastry, seal around edges.
7. Bake at 400 degrees for 20 minutes; cool slightly and serve.

Makes 6 to 8 servings.

1. To a large Dutch oven, add olive oil, onion and ground venison. Cook over medium heat until onion is tender; drain.

2. Add Italian stewed tomatoes, tomato paste, bell peppers, garlic granules, chili powder, and oregano to ground venison/onion mixture; simmer 25 minutes, stirring frequently.

3. Combine flour, baking powder and salt in a mixing bowl; stir. Cut in shortening and add milk; stir lightly until mixed.

4. Turn out pastry topping
   onto floured surface; roll
   out two thirds of topping
   to fit large baking dish.
   Form pastry shell to fit
   dish.

5. Pour venison/tomato
   mixture into pastry shell;
   sprinkle top evenly with
   mozzarella cheese.
   Top cheese with remaining
   dough, seal around edges.

6. Bake at 400 degrees for 20
   minutes. Remove from oven,
   cool slightly and serve.

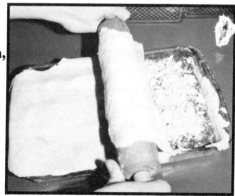

After a long day of hunting, cooking a difficult meal probably sn't on your list of favorite activities. So heat up the Dutch ven and throw in the following ingredients. By the time you've hanged into dry clothes, the chili will be ready to eat.

CHILI

2 tablespoons olive oil
2 pounds lean-ground venison
2 medium onions, chopped
1 medium bell pepper, chopped
2 cloves garlic, diced
2 (16-ounce) cans tomato sauce
2 (14 1/2-ounce) cans stewed tomatoes
1 teaspoon salt
1/2 teaspoon pepper
6 tablespoons chili powder

. Heat olive oil in Dutch oven; add lean-ground venison, onion, bell pepper and diced garlic, stirring to crumble meat.
. Cook over medium heat, continuing to stir, until onion is tender and ground venison is lightly browned; drain.
. Stir in tomato sauce, stewed tomatoes, salt, pepper and chili powder. Cover, reduce heat, and simmer 20 to 30 minutes, stirring occasionally.

Makes 8 servings.

Although there are dozens of specific spaghetti sauces to choose from in today's supermarkets, this homemade version goes well with the unique flavor of ground venison.

SPAGHETTI

2 tablespoons olive oil
1 pound lean-ground venison
1 medium onion, chopped
1 medium bell pepper, chopped
2 (14 1/2 ounce) cans stewed tomatoes, undrained
2 (6 ounce) cans tomato paste
1 teaspoon oregano
1 teaspoon basil
1/2 teaspoon garlic powder (more is optional)
hot cooked spaghetti
Parmesan cheese

1. Heat olive oil in Dutch oven; add ground venison, onion and bell pepper, stirring to crumble venison.
2. Cook over medium heat, stirring often, until onion is tender and venison is browned.
3. Stir in stewed tomatoes, tomato paste, oregano, basil and garlic powder; cover, reduce heat, and simmer 30 minutes, stirring occasionally.
4. Pour sauce over hot-cooked spaghetti and sprinkle with Parmesan cheese.
5. Serve with garden salad and browned garlic bread.

Makes 4 servings.

With dietary guidelines recommending we reduce our fat intake, the time is right for a low-fat goulash using lean-ground venison as the meat base.

GOULASH

1 pound lean-ground venison
2 teaspoons olive oil
1 medium bell pepper, chopped
1 medium onion, chopped
2 (14 1/2 ounce) cans stewed tomatoes, undrained
1/2 teaspoon salt
1/2 teaspoon coarse-ground black pepper
3 cups hot-cooked macaroni

1. Heat olive oil in Dutch oven, add ground venison, bell pepper and onion; cook over medium heat stirring often to crumble until venison is browned on all sides.
2. Add bell pepper and onion, stirring often, until bell pepper and onion are tender, about 5 minutes.
3. Stir in 1 can stewed tomatoes, salt, coarse-black pepper and macaroni; cover, and cook 25 minutes.
4. Stir in remaining can of stewed tomatoes and simmer 5 minutes.

Makes 4 servings.

When the occasion demands something a little different, try these palate-pleasing venison rolls topped with cranberry glaze and garnished with fresh chives or green onions.

VENISON ROLLS

2 tablespoons olive oil
1 pound lean-ground venison
1 cup chives, diced
1/2 cup green bell pepper, diced
1 teaspoon salt
1/4 teaspoon black pepper, table grind
2 tablespoons flour
1 cup milk
2 cups flour
4 teaspoons baking powder
1 teaspoon salt
3 tablespoons shortening
3/4 cup milk
butter

1. Heat olive oil in medium skillet; add ground venison, chives, bell pepper, salt and pepper. Cook over medium heat until venison is browned, stirring frequently to crumble; drain.
2. Stir in 2 tablespoons flour; add milk and cook until mixture is thick and bubbly. Remove from heat and set aside.
3. Combine 2 cups flour, baking powder, salt, shortening and milk in mixing bowl; stir until mixed well.
4. Roll out mixed dough to 1/4-inch thick; brush top evenly with melted butter.
5. Spread buttered top evenly with meat mixture; roll up like a jelly roll and cut into 1 1/4 to 1 1/2-inch thick slices.
6. Place slices in oiled baking dish; bake in preheated 400-degree oven for 20 to 25 minutes or until rolls are lightly browned.

Makes 4 to 6 servings.

If you're looking for a new twist for dinner, you may want to try stuffed peppers as the main course. Fresh bell peppers seem to complement the flavor of lean-ground venison.

STUFFED PEPPERS

8 large bell peppers
1/4 teaspoon salt
1 pound lean-ground venison
2 cups cooked white or brown rice
1 teaspoon chili powder
1 teaspoon garlic salt
1 1/2 teaspoons coarse black pepper
2 tablespoons minced onion
2 (14 1/2 ounce) cans Italian stewed tomatoes, undiluted
1 cup mozzarella cheese, grated

. Cut the top out of each bell pepper; remove seeds and rinse.
. In a large sauce pan, add 1/4 teaspoon salt and enough water to
  cover bell peppers. Parboil for 6 minutes:drain and set aside.
. Combine venison, cooked rice, chili powder, garlic salt, pepper,
  minced onion, and 1 can Italian stewed tomatoes in large skillet;
  stir well. Simmer until venison is mostly cooked through; drain.
. Spoon mixture evenly into parboiled bell peppers; arrange
  peppers in a lightly-oiled shallow baking dish.
. Top with 1 can tomatoes and mozzarella cheese; bake in
  preheated 375-degree oven for 25 minutes.

Makes 8 servings.

1. Cut the top out of each
   bell pepper; remove seeds
   and rinse.

2. In a large sauce pan, add 1/4 teaspoon salt and enough water to cover bell peppers. Parboil for 6 minutes:drain and set aside.

3. Combine venison, cooked rice, chili powder, garlic salt, pepper, minced onion and 1 can stewed tomatoes in large skillet; stir well. Simmer until venison is cooked through; drain.

4. Spoon mixture evenly into parboiled bell peppers; arrange peppers in a lightly-oiled shallow baking dish. Top with 1 can stewed tomatoes and mozzarella cheese; bake in preheated 375-degree oven for 25 minutes.

My wife inherited this wonderful stroganoff recipe from her favorite grandmother and has since adapted it to suit the unique flavor of venison. Add a simple side of corn-on-the-cob and fresh-baked rolls to make the meal complete.

STROGANOFF

2 tablespoons butter
1 pound lean ground venison
1 cup onion, diced
1 (8 oz.) can mushroom stems and pieces, drained
2 tablespoons flour
2 teaspoons garlic salt
1/4 teaspoon pepper
1 (10 3/4 oz.) can cream of chicken soup
1 cup sour cream
4 cups cooked noodles
Fresh parsley

1. Heat butter in large skillet; add ground venison, onion and mushrooms. Cook over medium heat until venison is browned, stirring frequently to crumble; drain.
2. Stir in flour, garlic salt, pepper and cream of chicken soup; cook over medium-low heat 8 minutes, stirring frequently.
3. Stir in sour cream; heat through.
4. Garnish with fresh parsley sprigs and serve over hot cooked noodles.

Makes 4 servings.

After a hectic day at work the last thing you want to do when you get home is get involved in a difficult recipe. Try this for simplicity and great taste.

OLD-FASHIONED MEAT LOAF

1 1/2 cup seasoned croutons
1 1/4 cup milk
2 eggs, beaten
2 pounds lean-ground venison
1 medium white or yellow onion, diced
1/2 cup catsup
1 teaspoon salt
1/8 teaspoon black pepper, table grind
Vegetable cooking spray, butter flavored
6 strips lean bacon

1. Combine croutons, milk and eggs in ample-size mixing bowl; soak 1 to 2 minutes.
2. Add ground venison, onion, catsup, salt and pepper to crouton mixture; mix well.
3. Spray loaf pan with butter flavored vegetable spray, place ground venison mixture into loaf pan; shape into loaf.
4. Bake loaf in preheated 350-degree oven for 30 minutes; add bacon strips evenly to top of loaf, bake an additional 30 minutes or until loaf is cooked through.

Makes 8 servings.

*Prevent supper-time doldrums by building your next evening
meal around a big platter of old-fashioned Venison Porcupine
Balls. Finicky eaters will likely be clamoring for more.*

PORCUPINE BALLS

2 pounds lean-ground vension
8 slices white bread, cubed
2 eggs beaten
2 cups milk
1 large red onion, diced
2 stalks celery, diced
2 cups cabbage, shredded
2 cups cooked rice
2 teaspoons salt
olive oil
2 cups tomato juice
1 (14 1/2 ounce) can stewed tomatoes, undrained

1. Place ground venison, bread, eggs, milk, onion, celery, cabbage,
   cooked rice and salt in large mixing bowl; mix together well.
2. Brush ample-size casserole dish with a light coating of
   olive oil.
3. Roll venison/bread mixture into 8 balls and place into lightly oiled
   casserole dish.
4. Pour tomato juice over meat (porcupine) balls and bake
   45 minutes in preheated 350-degree oven, or until porcupine
   balls reach desired degree of doneness.
5. Pour stewed tomatoes evenly over porcupine balls; cook
   another 5 minutes.

Makes 8 servings.

If your family's tired of traditional-type burgers, try this recipe. Different and delicious!

BARBECUED BURGERS

1 to 2 tablespoons olive oil
2 pounds lean-ground venison
1 cup green onions, chopped
1/2 cup green bell peppers, diced
1 (8 ounce) can mushroom stems and pieces, drained
1 (6 ounce) can tomato paste
1 (14 1/2 ounce) can Italian-style stewed tomatoes
2 tablespoons brown sugar
2 tablespoons cider vinegar
1 teaspoon prepared mustard
1 teaspoon Worcestershire sauce
1 teaspoon table salt
8 lightly-browned hamburger rolls

1. Heat olive oil in large-size skillet; add ground venison. Cook over medium heat, stirring often to crumble, until venison is browned; drain.
2. Stir in green onions, green bell peppers, mushroom stems and pieces; cook over medium heat until onions are fork tender.
3. Add tomato paste, stewed tomatoes, brown sugar, cider vinegar, mustard, Worcestershire sauce and salt; stir until mixed well.
4. Simmer over medium-low heat 20 minutes, stirring occassionally.
5. Serve with lightly-browned hamburger rolls.

Makes 8 servings.